Splitting and Projective Identification

CLASSICAL PSYCHOANALYSIS AND ITS APPLICATIONS

A Series of Books
Edited by Robert Langs, M.D.

Splitting
and Projective
Identification

James S. Grotstein

JASON ARONSON
NEW YORK • LONDON

ISBN: 0-87668-348-0

Library of Congress Catalog Number: 79-51928

10 9 8 7 6 5 4 3 2 1

Manufactured in the United States of America

Contents

Preface

Now that classical analytic authors are extending their interest, curiosity, and researches from the level of oedipal neurosis back to the earlier and deeper levels of narcissism, they are running into a wealth of discoveries which have already been surveyed by Melanie Klein and her co-workers, as well as by Fairbairn, Winnicott, Balint, and others who comprise the "English school of object relations." Their own investigations, in turn, were subsequent to those of Abraham, Freud, Tausk, and Federn even earlier.

In order to comprehend the early state of mind, we need an understanding of the mental organization and the world view which characterizes it. This volume is an attempt to formulate a theory of this inchoate state by describing the origin and development of its two principal architects, splitting and projective identification. It is my hope that I can cast more light on the operation of these mechanisms and illustrate their unique roles in early personality development. In so doing, I shall try to discriminate between normal and abnormal aspects of splitting and of projective identification, and I shall also try to show how they cooperate with as well as oppose one another . By demonstrating that they are identical, I shall also attempt to put to rest the alleged differences between projection and projective identification.

Perhaps a word should be said about my choice of priorities

of subjects, that is, my choice to present *splitting* first and *projective identification* second. For many years my own particular interest lay clinically in projective identification. This book began as an attempt to explicate its intricacies definitively. I gradually came to realize, however, that splitting mechanisms have been taken too much for granted, not only by me, but by most analysts, so I decided to reassess my views and appraisals of splitting. Its priority in this book testifies to the result of my deliberation. Yet it should be borne in mind that one can rarely speak of one without the other.

I feel constrained to admonish the reader that he may find my language to be an admixture of familiarity and of strangeness. I hope to make those readers who are familiar with classical psychoanalytic language feel at home, and I hope also to offer hospitality to those more familiar with the concepts of Klein, Fairbairn, Winnicott, and especially Bion, who has been the greatest inspiration behind this volume. Ultimately, I have been trying to employ the language of experience, both conscious and unconscious, so as to bring greater clarity to the actual clinical events which are involved with splitting and projective identification. By the language of experience I include all aspects of phenomenology including feelings, imagination, imagery, and inference—otherwise known collectively as *phantasies*—to be distinguished from the language of mechanistic description or formal thought. When Mahler talks of the periods of autism, symbiosis, and separation-individuation, and when Kernberg talks of "pleasurable and unpleasurable self-object images," I shall try to supplement their descriptive language with Klein's phenomenological conception of the paranoid-schizoid and depressive positions. I hope by the reconciliation between these two languages, the language of formal description and the phenomenological language of experience, a third stereoscopically meaningful and significant language of achievement will emerge.

Acknowledgments

This volume owes much to the Interdisciplinary Group for Advanced Studies in Psychotic, Borderline, and Narcissistic Disorders, a group consisting of interested and devoted colleagues, all of whom are psychoanalysts or psychoanalytically influenced. They bring skills other than just psychoanalysis to bear on the problems of psychosis. One of them is a biochemist in addition to being an analyst; another is also a neurophysiologist; still another is a distinguished clinical psychologist who is well published in the field of schizophrenia; yet another is a professor of immunology at a local medical school. Three of our group have established a Department for Psychoanalytic Studies at Del Amo Hospital, Torrance, California, where ongoing research concerns the psychoanalytic approach to the treatment of psychotic cases with the use of therapist-manager teams.

The ideas presented in this volume are my own but they have gestated in a marvelous hatchery. The group members are: Ira Carson, M.D.; Ned Cowan, M.D.; Duke Fisher, M.D.; Ivan Gabor, M.D.; Bernard Hellinger, M.D.; James Hughes, M.D.; Michael Paul, M.D.; Lisa Pomeroy, Ph.D; William Rickles, M.D.; David Shoemaker, B.S.; Gary Trump, Ph.D.; Alfred Silver, M.D.; Frederick Vaquer, M.D.; and Allan Weiner, M.D. To them all I owe a debt of gratitude.

I am indebted also to my three personal analysts—Dr.

Robert Jokl (my training analyst), Dr. Ivan McGuire, and Dr. Wilfred Bion—for introducing me to classical psychoanalysis, the object relations school, to Klein, and to myself. I wish to express special gratitude to Dr. Bion for introducing me to *my* language of experience and helping me to hope I may yet acquire *my* language of achievement. To Dr. Albert Mason I am indebted for his supervision and instruction in the Kleinian viewpoint of splitting and projective identification, and although I was trained as a classical psychoanalyst, my experiences with Drs. Bion and Mason have left me in even deeper awe of the fundamental importance of these phenomena in psychoanalysis. I now consider it impossible to do analysis without them. In that regard I must acknowledge my debt to Freud and to Klein. More personally, I am indebted to my closer contact with the latter's followers for their suggestions in supervisory contacts over the years; among them, in addition to Bion and Mason, are Betty Joseph, Donald Meltzer, Herbert Rosenfeld, Hanna Segal, Hans Thorner, and John Wisdom. I am also indebted to my dear friend, the late Harry Guntrip, for putting me in contact with the importance of Fairbairn's concept of splitting, and I have more lately been considerably influenced by Kohut's new emphasis upon the psychology of the self. As the reader of this volume will see, I endeavor to place Kohut's work in a dual-track complementarity with the work of Klein.

I am particularly indebted to Dr. Robert Langs for his painstaking editorial comments on the first draft of "Projective Identification," for his encouragement that I should supplement it with a study of "Splitting," and finally for his laborious and diligent review of the whole of the present text. My gratitude is boundless to Dr. Frederick Vaquer for his painstaking proofreading and advice to me on the complete text. His was a monumental task, and I shall never forget his help.

I am eternally grateful to my wife and to my children for their encouragement, patience, and sacrifices. Without them I could not have gotten this work off the ground. I am also grateful to my secretary, Mrs. Cheryl Cole, for her diligence and loyalty, and to the late Mr. Peter A. Tararin, the Research Librarian of the Los Angeles Psychoanalytic Society and Institute, for his painstaking efforts in researching the bibliography.

Splitting
and Projective
Identification

Part One

Splitting

"I thus drew steadily nearer to that truth, by whose partial discovery I have been doomed to such dreadful shipwreck: that man is not truly one, but truly two. I say two, because the state of my knowledge does not pass beyond that point. Others will follow, other will outstrip me on the same lines; and I hazard the guess that man will ultimately be known for a mere polity of multifarious, incongrous and independent denizens."
Dr. Jekyll and Mr. Hyde

1

Splitting: A Fundamental Concept

Splitting denotes both a universal phenomenon which occurs throughout our daily lives in multifarious ways and a fundamental defense mechanism. It may be defined as *the activity by which the ego discerns differences within the self and its objects, or between itself and objects.* In the perceptual or cognitive sense, an act of discriminative separation is involved, while in the defensive sense splitting implies an unconscious phantasy by which the ego can split itself off from the perception of an unwanted aspect of itself, or can split an object into two or more objects in order to locate polarized, immiscible qualities separately. The ego can also split the internal perception of the relationship of objects to one another, or can experience the self as being split or fragmented by a force believed to be either within or beyond the self. This is the usage, as I hope to demonstrate in the review of the literature (chapter 2), which Freud and many of his followers had in mind.

The concept of splitting has had an interesting history in psychoanalysis. Nineteenth century psychiatrists referred to it as "double consciousness," and in *Studies in Hysteria* Breuer and Freud (1893–1895) termed it "double conscience," a phenomenon which seemed to obtain in all their cases. While Freud paid great attention to it at first, frequently referring to "splitting of consciousness," the use of the concept splitting was soon eclipsed, with the ascent of the impulse-defense psychology, by

3

repression. The mystery of "double consciousness" was secularized, its demonic connotations lost in what ultimately evolved as the "id" of structural theory. Although at the end of his life Freud returned to the study of splitting, it was not until the current interest in narcissism, highlighted by the works of Heinz Kohut and Otto Kernberg, that the analytic world generally was to take note of this concept. By that time, however, Melanie Klein, along with W. R. D. Fairbairn, had utilized splitting as a basis upon which to posit a whole new extension of psychoanalysis.

Splitting can be thought of as a mental mechanism on one hand and as an experience—or as a way of experiencing or *not* experiencing experiences—on the other hand. The experiencing of experiences normally requires the separation or splitting of the object of experience from the background experience. This distinction, so necessary in cognitive and perceptual psychology, depends on the ego's capacity to distinguish *figure* from *ground* and then to distinguish further subqualities and quantifications of the object. This capacity to distinguish the objects of experience is based upon the principle of distinction, which owes its origin to the ego's inchoate capacity to split. Normal splitting has an epigenesis. The ego's capacity to split objects of perception depends on the infant's capacity to accept the *passive* experience of primal splitting, the act of birth separation. Once this primal splitting is accepted, the infant can then *actively* conduct perceptual (and later, cognitive) splittings of his object world.

Defensively, splitting can be thought of as active or passive. Active splitting of the self and of the object is intentional, whether consciously or unconsciously, whereas passive splitting seems to "happen" to one as the experience of a fragmentational confrontation with an overwhelming reality. In the clinical situation, it may be difficult both for the patient and the analyst to tell the difference between the active and passive aspects of defensive splitting, particularly when they are excessive.

One can see the zonal stages of development as participants

in this epigenesis of splitting. In the oral stage, the teeth actively separate one part of the object from another, and the sense organs follow in train in being able to separate aspects of the object in space. In the anal stage, body content is separated from the self, and, later, feces are re-cognized as irrelevant residues to be split-off (separated) from the assimilated food. In the phallic stage, the genital organs are counterposed to their opposites in terms of parents and siblings, and thus a distinction is made between sexual identities.

THE RELATIONSHIP BETWEEN SPLITTING, REPRESSION (PRIMAL AND SECONDARY), AND OBJECT RELATIONS

Normal splitting, whether perceptual-cognitive, phenomenological, or defensive, depends on a link to an object. As I hope to show later, Bion's (1957a) conception of *the container and the contained* is a model for an object helping the infant to sort out (split into more utilizable components) those aspects of communication which are at first inchoately emotional. The parent, in other words, helps the infant to transform experience of organismic panic (Greenacre 1941, Mahler 1968, Mahler, Pine, and Bergman 1975) into signal anxiety for adaptive preparation to future dangers. Pathologically, a patient may experience himself or herself to be fragmented (pathologically split) because of a failure to have acquired a sense of self from an empathically protective and supportive object(s). The borderline and psychotic patient, for instance, may believe his skin boundary to be unable to hold himself in and may define himself by virtue of an undeveloped sense of self-boundary—all the legacy of an inadequate or defective experience of parenting (whether actual or phantasied). Thus, pathological splitting, whether experienced as active or passive, predicates a poor background support object. Sandler (1960) has referred to this as environmental safety, and Winnicott (1963) refers to it as the environmental mother as distinguished from the object mother. Kohut (1971, 1977) refers to a similar concept as the self-object.

In other publications (Grotstein 1979c,d,e,f, 1980b,c,d,e) I have referred to this concept as the Background Object of Primary Identification.

In chapter 6 I shall define at greater length the specific role of the Background Object of Primary Identification as one of three distinct self-objects. In the meanwhile, I hope it suffices to say that normal splitting—cognitive, phenomenological, or defensive—is a narcissistic luxury bequeathed by an empathic self-object which serves as a background of safety for the infant and helps it symbiotically to experience its own separation (primal splitting) safely from the background object and, further, to conduct splittings "in front," so to speak, in the field of perceptual view. *Primal repression,* therefore, can just as easily be called *primal splitting* insofar as it is a bond or guarantee between the nascent self and its protective object for the latter to contain, filter, dilute, or to diminish the former's experience so that the ability to exist in the world is made easier. Thus, the facilitating environment (Winnicott) is necessary so that the infant may be able to experience a tension control and be able to focus on urgent need priorities and be able to postpone other feelings.

At first, therefore, splitting is experienced as a vertical phenomenon insofar as the infant is able to separate one feeling from another, such as good feelings and bad feelings. As trust in object constancy develops, the infant is enabled to utilize the object as a reservoir or container of its temporarily postponed feelings (Bion 1957a). The acquisition of object constancy in the depressive position of separation-individuation (rapprochement subphase) allows for a shift from a vertical splitting to a horizontal one which is also accompanied by a topographical layering of consciousness-unconsciousness, at which time repression proper succeeds splitting.

THE NEUROLOGICAL BASIS FOR SPLITTING

Interestingly enough, splitting may not be merely a mental phenomenon alone but may have a parallel in the neurophysiological development of the central nervous system. Gazzaniga and LeDoux (1978), among others, have found that the corpus callosum and the deep cerebral commissures which unite the two cerebral hemispheres do not begin to myelinate (and therefore to function) until about three to four months of age, and do not complete myelination until adolescence. Klein's (1940) assignment of the depressive position to the third or fourth months postnatally, and Mahler's (1971) assignment of the hatching phase to the fifth month, bears an interesting correlation to this finding. The upshot of Gazzaniga's and LeDoux's researches are that, neurophysiologically *and* phenomenologically, the individual seems to experience two separate consciousnesses as well as brains for processing the data of experience, one which is sensory, objective, abstract, and neurophysiological, and the other which is spatial, subjective, primitive, and phantasy-oriented. (McLaughlin 1978) assigns primary process to the right brain and secondary process to the left brain.

The ultimate importance of Gazzaniga's and LeDoux's findings for our purposes is that they help us to understand that inborn splitting may be a method for achieving anesthesia of experience by keeping the two brain-minds from communicating with each other too quickly. Having two brain-minds to process data separately with a minimum of communication between them suggests that the impact of experience may be mitigated or deadened through a lack of depth or third dimensionality, so to speak. The slow coming together of the connections between the two brain-minds allows for a slow development of stereoscopic binocularization neurophysiologically, tantamount to the acquisition of the depressive position of separation-individuation with phenomenological reconciliation. It would be interesting to speculate whether those infants who are fated for later borderline and psychotic illnesses may have suffered an infantile catastrophe because of a precocious development of the binocularizing commissures. (Grotstein 1979a,b, 1980d,e)

THE CATEGORIES OF DEFENSES

In other contributions (Grotstein 1980b,c,d,e) I have attempted to distinguish those defenses which epigenetically descend from the infantile neurosis from those which descend from an infantile psychosis. I believe that the infantile neurosis begins with the paranoid-schizoid position (autistic and symbiotic phases) and employs the psychical mechanisms of splitting, projective identification, magic omnipotent denial, and idealization. It is followed by the depressive position of separation-individuation which is characterized by the employment of the mechanisms of introjection, identification, unification, reconciliation, manic defenses, repression, and the derivatives of repression. Thus, the infantile neurosis accounts for the epigenesis from splitting to repression and is characterized by the organizing phenomenon of postponement (insofar as neurotic mechanisms allow it).

The infantile psychosis, on the other hand, is characterized by a disavowal of mental experience *and* the mind which experiences the experience (Bion 1959a). Psychotic defenses, as distinguished from neurotic defenses, are aimed at the annihilation of experience and the capacity to experience experience; thus, there is no postponement to the future but rather an eradication of the past and the future through the mechanisms of disavowal, negation, or negative hallucination. (Peto 1977) The splitting and projective identification which are organized by the infantile neurosis and its capacity to postpone are fundamentally different from the splitting and projective identification organized under the aegis of the infantile psychosis and its tendency to disavow the future and the past. Splitting and projective identification in these instances are very costly to self-cohesiveness, are rigid or amorphous, often violent and extreme, and promote even more abnormal states of mindlessness. They always denote a lack of a background object of safety (a deficient self-object experience) and therefore a failure to transform organismic panic into signal anxiety.

SPLITTING AS A DEFENSE

Melanie Klein was so impressed by the centrality of the life and death instincts in mental life, and their interaction, that she postulated that the infant needed to keep them separate and split apart from one another. Her observations of infants and her experience in the new field of child psychoanalysis, which she helped to found, convinced her of an earlier origin of the opedipus complex than was generally accepted. She was actually able to fathom an infantile internal world which was well established long before the genital-oedipal internal world. This world was characterized by phantasmal elaborations of objects which were created by projective identifications (generalizations of the self onto the object through the principle of similarities), thereby forming good and bad internal images of external objects. Splitting, the ancestor of repression, became necessary, she believed, in order to help keep separate these two classes of internal objects.

Splitting as a defense constitutes a phantasy whereby the subject may experience being split, or else experience a splitting in the object which confronts him. The motive for splitting in the former instance might be some need to discriminate between pleasure and unpleasure, pain and comfort, goodness and badness, etc. The case for splitting the object, on the other hand, derives from a readiness for ambivalence to develop in the infant: it becomes necessary to distinguish between the pleasure-giving qualities and the pain of frustration caused by the selfsame object. A need therefore emerges to distinguish between two separate beings within one parental object, and it is this survival necessity which instigates splitting the object, originally into what Klein (1921) described as the "good breast" and the "bad breast."

Pathologically, splitting involves separating experience, or the self which experiences the experience. Pathological splitting also alters the perception of the object by inappropriate divisions, by splintering and fragmentation. Splitting the perception of an object is also associated with a splitting of the self, divided along lines comparable to a cleavage in the object. Thus, the infant can split his primary object into a good object and a bad object; these split-off objects are thereafter related to by split-off selves which correspond to identifications with relative perceptions of the objects. The act of splitting may be active or experienced as passive, and we can speak of macroscopic and microscopic splitting. Macroscopic splitting refers to such phenomena as dissociation of personality, whereas microscopic splitting is more subtle and may appear in many different forms.

One of the most common examples of splitting in the therapeutic situation occurs between the patient's internalized image of the analyst and the analyst himself. When a patient who has "acted out" on a weekend, for example, comes into a Monday morning session, there frequently is a split between the internal analyst who has been with the patient all weekend, and the real analyst who has yet to hear what the patient has been up to.

Melanie Klein conceived of splitting originating as a defense which utilizes the energy of the death instinct, and from this premise she developed the idea of early mental life formed by phantasies employing *schizoid mechanisms,* characterized by the experience of paranoid anxiety. At firt she called this the *schizoid position* and later, adopting Fairbairn's conception, the *paranoid-schizoid position* (Klein 1946). The schizoid defenses included not only splitting, but also projective identification, idealization, and magic omnipotent denial, all of which are employed to protect the infant from feelings of persecution by bad objects. Schizoid mechanisms, according to Klein, enable the infant to split off and to project or omnipotently master bad objects by transposing them from the inside of the psyche to the outside.

Insofar as the schizoid mechanisms are never completely successful, the infant experiences not only a projective riddance of the object but also an identification with the object into which he has projected his bad object. This can best be imagined by seeing the process of splitting and projective identification in

sequence: *(a)* the splitting-off of a bad object from consciousness (e.g., hunger as a bad breast), which then is projected
outward into an external object; *(b)* the introjection of the result
of this transaction, so that the projected-into object is now
internalized and occupies a position in the infant's internal
world. The infant now contains a split-off portion of himself
encased in an object. This "layering" phenomenon, according
to Klein (1946), is the epitome of the schizoid state.

It is important to note that defensive splitting, as conveyed by
the term *split off,* always involves the auxiliary participation of
projective identification in order to translocate the split-off
aspect of the personality. Thus, in infancy and childhood, when
there is difficulty in establishing a clear-cut, discrete internal
world, the unconscious experience of being split predicates a
high degree of identification with objects into which the splits
are projected. The infant's sense of "oneness" may be spread
across many objects.

The significance of defensive splitting lies in the experience of
confronting alienated aspects of oneself. "Split-off" really
means that a part of one's being has undergone alienation,
mystification, mythification, and re-personification—in effect,
has become someone else, an alien presence within. The terms
"impulse," "drive," and "part of self" are all inadequate to
express the profundity of this experience. The term "compulsion," which really is an impulse of the superego, comes closer.
Defensive splitting is an act of the imagination which bequeaths
to the split-off portions of the personality a life-support system
with the will to live, which then repersonifies this creation in a
way that it might as well be thought of as someone else—were it
not that some unconscious, mysterious connection, much like
déjà vu, persists to cause the splitter the agony of being haunted
by a split which he can neither remember nor forget!

Extreme splitting, as seen in borderline and psychotic cases,
can be likened to a medieval state comprised of many feudal
lords loosely bonded in a fiefdom by a tentative monarchy.
When the monarchy is weakened or deposed, the feudal lords
go contumaciously and independently about their several pur-

poses. This can be observed in analytic practice when one hears free associations which approximate or become loose associations that seem to be montages of speech from multiple subpersonalities seemingly talking all at once. Borderline and psychotic patients, because of the defective repressive barrier, may demonstrate more active dissociation of personality where there is either a mutual incompatibility between the splits, or a proliferation of multiple split personalities which seemingly exist together without contradiction.

SOME CLINICAL EXAMPLES

There are, I have concluded, two general categories of splitting: the experience of splitting and the splitting of experience. The former can be thought of as the experience of being split, while the latter represents the active function of splitting off the experience. Our sense of primal at-one-ment (primary identification) receives its first blow with mental birth, which may be experienced as a divisive thrust from pristine serenity. This first experience of separation from the state of primary identification is elaborately repeated in many analytic hours. For psychotic and borderline patients, it is commonly experienced as a mutilation of at-one-ment; here is an example from a more neurotic case.

A twenty-five-year-old single female entered analysis after terminating another long analysis which had been successful in many ways but not in terms of her intimate object relations. After a weekend break the patient reported associations which suggested a highly erotic transference to me. At the same time, she stated that she could not stand to wait for the next analytic hour and therefore had eaten an enormous number of cookies at the place where she worked. As she was eating, she had imagined each cookie to be a "little Grotstein." At first she felt filled up with me, but later felt bad because she had a weight problem and knew that the cookies were not good for her. Later, as she approached her home, she longed for someone to be waiting for her with a hot meal. Then she became sad and called her mother, who was living in a distant city; she told her mother how much she loved and missed her.

I interpreted to the patient that she had felt good about the last analytic hour and wished that it would not end, because ending meant to her that she felt split off from me, and by me, into a cold separateness. She was then occupied by a desperate wish (greed) to bypass the split-off state of separation, and to incorporate me instead, by an omnipotent and idealized appointment with the cookies (splitting off the experience of being split off). Since these were omnipotent, handy, spurious objects under her control and not really an experience with me, she felt stuffed and bad, as though she had tried in vain to evacuate (split off) the feeling of longing by telling herself she was stuffing herself with me (confusion between incorporation and evacuation). Then, I continued, she was able to experience that what she did on her own was not good enough, and she came into contact with the awareness of the need for the nurturing breast rather than the evacuative, exciting one used for amnesia.

Her response to my interpretation was an acknowledgment of its correctness. She then recalled a dream she had over the weekend: she had a bowel movement in the woods in which there were two lumps of feces. She also recalled that in the dream her father was angry with her. Multiple associations to this dream ultimately led me to interpret that the two bowel movements were attempts to evacuate (split off) a conflict which consisted of her need to split her previous analyst and myself in a way parallel to her need to split her father from her mother. The bowel movement in the woods suggested her confirmation of my interpretation about being split off and left in the open with no one to take care of her evacuative needs over the weekend. The patient accepted this interpretation, and seemed to understand that her conflictual feelings seemed to center around various aspects of splitting.

A psychotic patient whose progress in analysis led him to want to return to his hometown, from which he had fled when he had his psychotic break, developed a series of splitting episodes which were characterized as follows. In proportion as he desired to return to his hometown, he split off his desire to follow his "grown-up" career in Los Angeles and to remain in analysis with me by projecting his greedy feelings into me, so that I was experienced as the one who did not want him to go back home and who was holding onto him for the money. When on the other hand he wanted to remain in Los Angeles to continue his analysis, he split off and projected into me those aspects which wanted to go back to his hometown in such a way that he believed I was in collusion with his father to send him back East because I wanted to be rid of him. What the patient was finally able to achieve, with analytic help, was a state of ambivalence in which he realized he had both wishes at the same time—a fact which presented him with the experience of unbearable conflict.

At this point I interpreted to him that he was now in contact with the belief that his needs had so damaged his mother and her breasts that he abolished the awareness of his needs by flattening them and by flattening the image of the breasts. He then banished them to his negative self to be permanently forgotten. Following this interpretation more memories began to emerge from the amnestic era.

Most analytic hours can be viewed as demonstrating the splitting of aspects of the self and of one's objects. A twenty-two-year-old patient dreamed that I came into her apartment to treat her roommate and not her. She was hurt and disappointed. Her associations led to the awareness that the roommate, whom she described as her own languid and dependent counterpart, was in contrast to her own more manifest personality, which was domineering, aggressive, and provocatively self-assertive. Her roommate depicted a split-off aspect of herself which represented a more passive and dependent self who was more aware of her need to be cared for. In all probability, all patient and dream material, although it may be viewed on many different levels of abstraction, may ultimately represent split aspects of the self in the first place, and split perceptions of one's objects secondarily.

My own experience with patients of all categories has convinced me that people in general find themselves existing in split states of mind. A neurotic woman who was just terminating her lengthy analysis with me commented that she now realized she had been "beside herself" all her life. She believed that she had been a "sleepwalker," somebody walking in a fog, out of contact with her general seenario. She asked poignantly, "Did I really experience my life? Was I really there when my children were growing? Did I really experience my marriage to my husband? And did I really ever experience my analysis with you?"

SPLITTING AS A BASIC EGO MECHANISM

"It is splitting," Hanna Segal writes in her *Introduction to the Work of Melanie Klein* (1964),

which allows the ego to emerge out of chaos and to order its experiences. This ordering of experience which occurs with the process of splitting into a good and bad object, however excessive and extreme it may be to begin with, nevertheless orders the universe of the child's emotional and sensory impressions and is a precondition of later integration. It is the basis of what is later to become the faculty of discrimination, the origin of which is the early differentiation between good and bad. There are other aspects of splitting which remain and are important in mature life. For instance, the ability to pay attention, to suspend one's emotion in order to form an intellectual judgment, would not be achieved without the capacity for temporary reversible splitting. (p. 35)

Splitting is the primal detour the infant follows in the attempt to cope with the realization of the consequences of birth-separation and the ambivalence toward the objects of the newborn world—a detour necessitated by the immaturity of the perceptual apparatus and the paucity of defensive techniques to cope with sensation and perception. It may be defensive insofar as splitting facilitates the ego in disavowing any connection with what has been split off, but it also may be nondefensive.

Nondefensive splitting is useful is establishing perceptual and cognitive differentiations, and it represents adaptive, maturational growth insofar as it allows the infant to "bite" into the percept, so to speak, sort out the bits, and commit them to the digestive enzymes of internal experience, the forerunner of thinking. This active experience in the service of thinking and maturation probably follows the passive infant's inchoate experience of discontinuities of, or irruptions into, a harmonious sensorium—experienced, that is, as passive splitting or rents imposed upon the smooth symmetrical contour of the pre-birth harmony. This is the forerunner of consciousness and attention. Disturbing perturbations awaken the infant to the awareness of need and the necessity to adapt. It is a "turning on of the lights of life," so to speak, and of life's consequences.

Splitting normally runs a gamut: from the separation of self from object to the arbitrary separation of the object's content from container (biting, chewing, swallowing, etc.). Proceeding in epigenesis from passive to active along this continuum are alienation, premature closure, splintering, fragmentation, withdrawal, isolation, reaction-formation, phobia-formation, idealization, doing-undoing, and disengagement. The extensiveness of this list suggests, in fact, that splitting is, along with projective identification, one of the common denominators in all defense mechanisms. But it also suggests that splitting undergoes a maturation into more elaborate functions in normal development (and pathological alternations in abnormal development). Splitting thus undergoes the epigenesis of the modality of separation. It begins as a body-ego and body-image function. In the oral stage the infant must learn to bite, chew, and swallow, thus engaging his mouth in the activity of splitting the food content from the breast container, and also splitting the chosen food into even smaller fragments for swallowing—which introduces him to the loss of the object as it is internalized. Cannibalistic anxiety develops when the infant fears he has swallowed the chewed-up breast container. Food idiosyncrasies, the Kosher laws of the Jews, and the Eucharistic ceremony of the Christians, all reflect this cannibalistic anxiety. In the anal stage the child must learn the control of eliminative separation which, in phantasy, is the distinction between good feces and bad feces; and in the phallic-oedipal phase the sense of separate identities must be learned—the distinction between male and female. Thus, the epigenesis of splitting is the epigenesis of the quality of distinctiveness and capacity to separate qualities, both defensively and nondefensively.

In order for discrimination to occur, the sense organs conducting discriminating perceptions must themselves be divided (split) in order to offer different perspectives, so that correlation with the object of perception can occur. *Correlation* leads to perception in depth, and from that evolves the *significance* of the observation. Sense organs are naturally divided in order to achieve this discrimination. The finger opposes the thumb, one hand opposes the other, etc. The two eyes (or two ears, or two nostrils) perceive the same object from different vantage points and correlate their findings in higher cortical centers. The senses must also bring together sense data from their various vantage points in order to achieve "common sense" (Bion 1965). Splitting attacks the linkages of the senses, interdicts the achievement of common sense, and ultimately undermines the capacity to perceive and to think (Paul and Carson 1978). One can think of splitting as following the principle of distinction or differentiation (displacement), whereas projective identification follows the principle of generalization (condensation).

Splitting is also involved in macroscopic activities such as discriminations between inside and outside, sleep-wakefulness, and normal cyclic activities generally. It therefore emerges as an important component in ordering the sequences of activities, even to the extent of postponing the future. Bergman and Escalona (1949) hinted at this postponement phenomenon without actually mentioning splitting. They suggested that the infant has some access to his genetic future even at birth but is biologically able to postpone his awareness of it until he is age-specific for his appropriate identity tasks, such as achievement of the phallic-oedipal complex and adolescent sexuality. Splitting helps to order the sequence to permit postponement.

A BROAD FORMULATION

Splitting, then, is a basic mental mechanism which includes perceptual, cognitive, and defense operations. It is a universal experience of man and originates from the experience of existing in separate subselves or separate personalities which have never been totally unified into a single oneness. "At-one-ment" is not only the goal of analysis; it also is the goal of life. Yet it must remain only our aim, never our achievement. Perhaps the experience of being split is more nearly conscious in abnormal personalities who have not achieved a confident capacity to repress, but that is only another way of stating that those who have not achieved a normal resolution of the oedipus complex, with the legacy of a normal superego and the capacity for normal repression, will experience being split to a greater degree. Those who have achieved normal repression as a result of oedipal resolution, will experience unconscious splitting but will not have conscious experience of it. Normal personalities are split, but their experience of splitting is mitigated by repression.

The most common connotation of splitting, and the more generally understood, refers to the improper or unnatural separation of objects or selves, such as in the clinical examples quoted above. This usage, relating to the defensive uses of splitting, will be understood in the presentation that follows, unless otherwise designated. The genesis of the concept splitting in psychoanalysis, its appearance in the works of Freud and his followers and later in the thought of Melanie Klein and proponents of the object relations school, will be explored in the review of the literature, three chapters to which we now may turn.

2

Freud's Concepts of Splitting

Splitting of the psyche was of deep interest to novelists as well as scientists for several generations before the discovery of psychoanalysis. E. T. A. Hoffman, the German Romantic, was obsessed by the phenomenon of split personalities, and examples from nineteenth century literature include Dostoyevsky's *The Double,* Oscar Wilde's *Portrait of Dorian Gray,* and Robert Louis Stevenson's *Doctor Jekyll and Mr. Hyde.* Edgar Allen Poe's doppleganger tale, "William Wilson," and Adelbert von Chamisso's *Peter Schlemihls wundersame Geschichte,* the story of a man who sells his shadow to the devil, also fall within this tradition. Although we have lost sight of the fact because of Freud's deemphasis of splitting in favor of repression, psychoanalysis emerged, in part, from this atmosphere summoned by the theme that man contains within his darker nature a furtively impulsive and demonically impassioned self.

In a broad sense, Freud in his earliest studies started to establish a conception of man as having a conscious personality constantly beset by an unconscious personality created by the traumatic memory of an event in childhood—thereby challenging the conception of the unified personality and revealing it to be "split" in its fundamental nature. Somewhat later, his discovery that the traumatic memory from childhood was not of a real event but a phantasy, had a momentous impact on the history of psychoanalysis. It heralded the discovery of infantile sexuality, culminating in the oedipal conflict, and the instinctual drive theory. But this noteworthy change of emphasis also culminated in the secularization of the components of the unconscious from their earlier, demonic connotations. Freud abandoned his consideration of *double conscience* (the French term, which Freud and Breuer had adopted, for dual consciousness) in favor of a topographical theory in which the unconscious was subordinated by consciousness. Conscious, preconscious, and unconscious *(systems cs., pcs,* and *ucs.)* became psychic layers, horizontally more congruent with repression than with splitting (which had been "vertical" in the sense that each split was conscious). Thereafter, the history of psychoanalysis lay mainly in the study of those neuroses which evinced this horizontal and topographical (later structural) prejudice, as it were. It was not until 1927 in his paper on "Fetishism" that Freud returned to his earlier interest in separate states of mind which are split off and opposed to one another.

SPLITTING IN HYSTERIA

Fairbairn has called attention (1940, 1941) to the fact that Freud firmly laid the groundwork for the major significance of splitting in psychopathology by choosing to study an entity which so beautifully demonstrated it—hysteria. In "On the Psychical Mechanism of Hysterical Phenomena: Preliminary Communication," Breuer and Freud (1893–1895) discuss the origin of the hysterical symptoms in the early traumatic memory of patients.

> It is not possible to establish a point of origin by a simple interrogation of the patient . . . because what is in question is often some experience which the patient dislikes discussing; but principally because he is genuinely unable to recollect it and often has no suspicion of the causal connection between the precipitating event and the pathological phenomenon. (p. 3)

In discussing the case of Anna O, Breuer stated:

> Two entirely distinct states of consciousness were present which alternated very frequently and without warning, and which became more and more differentiated in the course of the illness. . . . At moments when her mind was quite clear she would complain of the profound darkness in her head, of not being able to think, of becoming blind and deaf, of having two selves, a real one and an evil one which forced her to behave badly, and so on. (p. 24)

Freud and Breuer were calling the altered states their patients experienced autohypnotic *absences*. For Anna O, Breuer wrote that

> the regular order of things was: the somnolent state in the afternoon, followed after sunset by the deep hypnosis for which she invented the technical name of 'clouds.' . . . It was a truly remarkable contrast: in the day-time the irresponsible patient pursued by hallucinations, and at night the girl with her mind completely clear. (pp. 27–28).

These secondary states of mind together comprised "a second state of consciousness which first emerged as a temporary *absence* and later became organized into a *'double conscience.'*" (p. 42), Breuer then suggested that

> in this secondary state the patient was in a condition of alienation. . . . It is hard to avoid expressing the situation by saying that the patient was *split* into two personalities of which one was mentally normal and the other insane. (p. 45; my italics)

Freud treated the case of Lucy R, which he regarded as a good example of traumatic etiology. Believing that intially an idea must have been excluded from consciousness for hysteria later to occur, Freud stated:

> The characteristic feature of (the) auxiliary moment (i.e., when the hysterical symptoms emerge) is, I believe, that the two

divided psychical groups temporarily converge in it, as they do in the extended consciousness which occurs in somnambulism. (p. 123; my italics)

At this point, as Pruyser has pointed out (1975), Freud held that *splitting of the content* of consciousness (i.e., not of consciousness) is the result of an act of will.

In the case of Elisabeth von R, Freud suggested that the strong resistance at work to prevent association of certain ideas provided the motive for the splitting of consciousness, with conversion the method.

In this way a transformation was effected which had the advantage that the patient escaped from an intolerable mental condition; though it is true, this was at the cost of a psychical abnormality—the *splitting of consciousness* that came about—and of the physical illness—her pains, on which an astasia-abasia was built up. (p. 166; my italics)

Freud held, as Pruyser has pointed out (1975) with respect to "The Neuro-Psychoses of Defence," for a splitting of consciousness accompanied by the formation of separate psychical groups, as if to suggest that these were two different things. Freud had greater regard for Breuer's propositions which gave splitting of consciousness a secondary place. The patient intended to split the content of consciousness, not consciousness itself, but according to Freud, the act backfired.

LATER FORMULATIONS

In the above quotations, Freud and Breuer seem to have conceived of psychopathology in hysteria as consisting of a split-off portion of a separate nuclear complex, either coexisting in consciousness or subordinated to it. The consequence was something of a "Jekyll and Hyde" concept of *"double conscience"* as typical of neurosis. The split-off complexes were considered hypnoid states and occurred in hysterics because of their supposed proclivity to them.

Freud did not entirely abandon this explanation in terms of dissociated states and in *Five Lectures on Psycho-Analysis* (1909) observed that

> the study of hypnotic phenomena has accustomed us to what was at first a bewildering realization that in one and the same individual there can be several mental groupings, which can remain more or less independent of one another, which can 'know nothing' of one another and which can alternate with one another in their hold upon consciousness. Cases of this kind, too, occasionally appear spontaneously, and are then described as examples of *'double conscience.'* If, where a splitting of the personality such as this has occurred, consciousness remains attached regularly to one of the two states, we call it the *conscious* mental state and the other, which is detached from it, the *unconscious* one. (p. 19)

The importance of splitting, however, as a more general mechanism was given up. In *On the History of the Psycho-Analytic Movement* (1914a), Freud states:

> I looked upon psychical splitting itself as an effect of a process of repelling which at that time I called 'defence', and later, 'repression'. I made a shortlived attempt to allow the two mechanisms a separate existence side by side, but as observation showed me always and only one thing, it was not long before my 'defence' theory took up its stand opposite his [Breuer's] 'hypnoid' one. (p. 11)

Splitting was thus enveloped in the larger term, *repression,* and stayed eclipsed for many years, even though it is the discernible concept at work, for example, in "Family Romances" (Freud 1908). In that paper, Freud delineated the universal fantasy in which children imagine that they have been born of wealthy, noble, or powerful parents who retreat into mystery soon afterward, leaving them in the care of loving servants. Although Freud does not use the term splitting for this phenomenon, he is nonetheless clearly indicating a cleavage between the conceptualization of the remote and proud parents on the one hand, and the low-born, but real parents on the other. In other contributions (Grotstein 1979a,b,c,g) and in chapter 10 of this book, I have used the concept of the split between the omnipotent parent and the real parent as a springboard to describe what I call the *background object of primary identification.*

Freud also made important discoveries about splitting in "On Narcissism: An Introduction" (1914b), in which he discussed the development of the ego-ideal as a split-off and projected aspect of the ego which becomes a separate agency which thereafter has an observing function. This idea was considerably elaborated in "Mourning and Melancholia" (Freud 1917b), in which splitting between the ego and ego-ideal took a more definitive form. The so-called melancholic, in whom self-criticism is outstanding, confronts the loss of a love object through identification; the lost object is installed in the ego.

> Thus the shadow of the object fell upon the ego, and the latter could henceforth be judged by a special agency, as though it were an object, the foresaken object. In this way an object-loss was transformed into an ego-loss and the conflict between the ego and the loved person into a cleavage between the critical activity of the ego and the ego as altered by identification. (p. 249)

The idea of a split between the ego and its ideal on one hand, and between the ego and its object on the other, was suggestive of a separate development for the narcissistic ego and the object relations ego—adumbrating the later work of Kohut. The object relations in depression regress to narcissistic object relations, which then devolve into a split, not between the ego and its objects in the external world, but rather between the ego identified with an object on one hand, and the ego-ideal identified with an object on the other. Freud's contribution to the theory of internal objects and their splits helped launch the schools of Klein and Fairbairn, from which today Kernberg and others descend.

In *The Ego and the Id* (1923), Freud stated:

we cannot avoid giving out attention for a moment longer to the ego's object-identifications. If they obtain the upper hand and become too numerous, unduly powerful and incompatible with one another, a pathological outcome will not be far off. It may come to a disruption of the ego in consequence of the different identifications becoming cut off from one another by resistances; perhaps the secret of the cases of what is described as 'multiple personality' is that the different identifications seize hold of consciousness in turn. Even when things do not go so far as this, there remains the question of conflicts between the various identifications into which the ego comes apart, conflicts which cannot after all be described as entirely pathological. (pp. 30–31)

Once again Freud is describing a conflict between the two basic subdivisions of the personality—the ego's relationship to its ideal and to its objects.

In his 1924 paper, "Neurosis and Psychosis," Freud dealt with the various ways in which the ego can resolve a conflict with either the id or the external world. "It will be possible," he writes, "for the ego to avoid a rupture in any direction by deforming itself, by submitting to encroachments on its own unity and even perhaps by effecting a cleavage or division of itself" (pp. 152–153).

It was in a famous, often quoted paper written in 1927, "Fetishism," that Freud returned specifically to the phenomenon of splitting, when he reaffirms its connection with two contradictory ideas about castration which are both conscious but split off from one another. In a clinical example he relates how

it turned out that the two young men had no more 'scotomized' their father's death than a fetishist does the castration of women. It was only one current in their mental life that had not recognized their father's death; there was another current which took full account of that fact. The attitude which fitted in with the wish and the attitude which fitted in with reality existed side by side. In one of my two cases this split had formed the basis of a moderately severe obsessional neurosis. The patient oscillated in every situation in life between two assumptions: the one, that his father was still alive and was hindering his activity; the other, opposite one, that he was entitled to regard himself as his father's successor. (p. 156)

Freud's statement of splitting in "Fetishism"—two states of mind, each of which is identified with an idea incompatible with the other—was to be used as his paradigm for the splitting processes in the ego by psychoanalysts thereafter.

In the *New Introductory Lectures on Psycho-Analysis* (1933) Freud establishes two major functions for splitting. He says:

> The ego can take itself as an object, treat itself like an object, can observe itself, criticize itself, and do heaven knows what with itself. In this, one part of the ego is setting itself over against the rest. So the ego can be *split;* it splits itself during a number of its functions—temporarily at least. . . . On the other hand, we are familiar with the notion that pathology, by making things larger and coarser, can draw out attention to normal conditions which would otherwise have escaped us. Where it points to a breach or a rent, there may normally be an articulation present. If we throw a crystal to the floor, it breaks; but not into haphazard pieces. It comes apart along its lines of cleavage into fragments whose boundaries, though they were invisible, were predetermined by the crystal's structure. Mental patients are split and broken structures of this same kind. (pp. 58–59)

Thus, in the normal, transient, reflective function of splitting, the ego can momentarily imagine itself its own object in order to promote its experiences; but pathologically, splitting denotes the permanent lines of cleavage, or fault lines, existing from the early development of the personality, which predicate future lines of cleavage.

Freud seems to have hinted at a continuity between splitting and fragmentation of the ego in *Moses and Monotheism* (1939), and splitting is the leading process. Writing of traumatic neurosis, Freud states:

> This . . . illness may also be looked upon as an attempt at cure— as an effort once more to reconcile with the rest of those portions

of the ego that have been split-off by the influence of the trauma and to unite them into a powerful whole vis-à-vis the external world. An attempt of this kind seldom succeeds, however, unless the work of analysis comes to its help, and even then not always; it ends often enough in a complete devastation or fragmentation of the ego or in its being overwhelmed by the portion which was early split off and which is dominated by the trauma. (pp. 77–78)

In the *Outline of Psycho-Analysis* (1940a), Freud discussed splitting as taking place in whole areas of the personality, implying a cleavage between normal and abnormal portions of the personality, which adumbrate the ideas of Katan (1954) and Bion (1967). Domination by the more incompatible split predicates psychosis.

one learns from patients after their recovery [from psychosis] that at the time in some corner of their mind (as they put it) there was a normal person hidden who, like a detached spectator, watched the hubbub of illness go past him. . . . We may probably take it as being generally true that what occurs in all these cases is a psychical *split*. Two psychical attitudes have been performed instead of a single one—one, the normal one, which takes account of reality, and another which under the influence of the instincts detaches the ego from reality. The two exist along side of each other. (p. 202)

Yet splitting of the ego also takes place in the neuroses, and Freud thereby establishes that it is a universal trend which occupies all psychopathology and has to do with lines of cleavage between incompatible groupings within an integrated ego.

The view which postulates that in all psychoses there is a *splitting of the ego* could not call for so much notice if it did not turn out to apply to other states more like the neuroses and, finally, to the neuroses themselves. I first became convinced of this in cases of *fetishism*. (p. 202)

Fetishism, continues Freud, is not exceptional but only a

particularly favorable example of splitting. "The childish ego," writes Freud,

> under the domination of the real world, gets rid of undesirable instinctual demands by what are called repressions. We will now supplement this by further asserting that, during the same period of life, the ego often enough finds itself in the position of fending off some demand from the external world which it feels distressing, and that this is effected by means of a *disavowal* of the perceptions which bring to knowledge this demand from reality. Disavowals of this kind occur very often and not only with fetishists; and whenever we are in a position to study them they turn out to be half-measures, incomplete attempts at detachment from reality. The disavowal is always supplemented by an aknowledgment; two contrary and independent attitudes always arise and result in the situation of there being a splitting of the ego. Once more the issue depends on which of the two can seize hold of the greater intensity.
>
> The facts of this splitting of the ego, which we have just described, are neither so new nor so strange as they may at first appear. It is indeed a universal characteristic of neuroses that there are present in the subject's mental life, as regards some particular behaviour, two different attitudes, contrary to each other and independent of each other. (pp. 203-204)

I have quoted Freud here at length in order to demonstrate his ultimate thesis, that splitting was not only a feature of psychosis and fetishism but was a common feature in the everyday lives of neurotics and is ubiquitous in infancy. Finally, he had given splitting the crucial importance it seemed clinically and theoretically to deserve. In his last commentary on the subject, "Splitting of the Ego in the Process of Defence" (1940b), Freud consolidated this view in a suggestive explanation of its genesis.

> Let us suppose, then, that a child's ego is under the sway of a powerful instinctual demand which it is accustomed to satisfy and that it is suddenly frightened by an experience which teaches it that the continuance of the satisfaction will result in an almost

intolerable real danger. It must now decide either to recognize the real danger, give way to it and renounce the instinctual satisfaction, or to disavow reality and make itself believe that there is no reason for fear, so that it may be able to retain the satisfaction. Thus there is a conflict between the demand by the instinct and the prohibition by reality. But in fact the child takes neither course, or rather he takes both simultaneously, which comes to the same thing. He replies to the conflict with two contrary reactions, both of which are valid and effective. . . . Both the parties to the dispute obtain their share: the instinct is allowed to retain its satisfaction and proper respect is shown to reality. (p. 275)

It is the concept of the "rift in the ego" which is to cast so important a shadow on all psychopathology, according to Freud. Strongly hinting that split states of mind continue as ego alterations, Freud emphasizes that the child can maintain the allegiance to his instinct and to reality in separate compartments, but would pay a price in terms of such pathological alteration of the ego.

By the time that Freud's interest in splitting was rekindled near the end of his life, Melanie Klein was already aware of its importance, and W. R. D. Fairbairn was shortly to make it the basis of his own metapsychology. It was to remain largely ignored by classical analysts for some years to come, but in the hands of Kleinians the next chapter in the history of the concept of splitting would ultimately become crucial for the entire field.

3

Klein's Concept

In *Envy and Gratitude,* a book written several years before her death, Melanie Klein discusses splitting at great length. "I have," she writes, "for many years attributed great importance to one particular process of splitting: the division of the breast into a good and bad object. I took this to be an expression of the innate conflict between love and hate and of the ensuing anxieties. However, coexisting with this division, there appeared various processes of splitting, and it is only in recent years that some of them have been more clearly understood" (1957, p. 23).

For Klein, as was not the case with Freud, splitting was an enduring concept throughout her work, as active in her later formulations as in her earliest. Assuming an ego operative from birth and infant anxiety to be related to the polarity of the life and death instincts, Klein, in her theory, described the early months of life as the *paranoid-schizoid position.* The term reflects the persecutory anxiety that besets the infant, as well as implies the defenses against it, splitting and projective identification. While splitting had been used by Klein as early as 1921, her later theory deepened its meaning and expanded its use. "For instance," she continues in *Envy and Gratitude,*

I found that concurrently with the greedy and devouring internalization of the object—first of all the breast—the ego in varying degrees fragments itself and its objects, and in this way achieves a dispersal of the destructive impulses and of internal persecutory anxieties. This process, varying in strength and determining the greater or lesser normality of the individual, is one of the defenses during the paranoid-schizoid position. . . .

. . . I take (the splitting process) to be a pre-condition for the young infant's relative stability; during the first few months he predominantly keeps the good object apart from the bad one and thus, in a fundamental way, preserves it—which also means the security of the ego is enhanced. At the same time, this primal division only succeeds if there is an adequate capacity for love and a relatively strong ego. My hypothesis is, therefore, that the capacity for love gives impetus both to integrating tendencies and to a successful primal splitting between the loved and hated object. This sounds paradoxical. But since, as I said, integration is based on a strongly rooted good object that forms the core of the ego, a certain amount of splitting is essential for integration; for it preserves the good object and later on enables the ego to synthesize the two aspects of it. Excessive envy, an expression of destructive impulses, interferes with the primal split between the good and bad breast, and the building up of a good object cannot sufficiently be achieved. (pp. 23-24)

The paranoid-schizoid position is succeeded by the *depressive position,* in which for the first time the infant comes to regard his mother as a whole object. Splitting and projective identification lessen, introjective mechanisms become more important, and anxiety due to ambivalence is paramount. If splitting in the previous position has not been so deep "as to inhibit integration," writes Klein in *Narrative of a Child Analysis,*

the foundation is laid for a growing capacity to distinguish between good and bad. This enables him during the period of the depressive position to synthesize in some measure the various aspects of the object. (p. 249)

Klein's *Narrative of a Child Analysis* (1960) was a posthumously published work in which a daily account of an analysis done at the beginning of World War II is evaluated some fifteen years later, in the light of her most advanced theory. The passage above highlights the importance of an identification with a good object so as to achieve normal splitting, and in a sense anticipates Heinz Kohut's "empathic psychology." Elsewhere in this monumental case history Klein also distinguishes various forms of splitting such as between the top and bottom of mother's body and between the front and the back—in effect, *planar splits*—the front dating to the distinction between nurture at the breast and excitement to contemplate or to enter mother's genitals, and the latter a distinction between excitement about mother's anus and rectum on one hand, and her genital on the other. And she also suggests that it is essential to distinguish between a good and an idealized object, and that

> a very deep split between the two aspects of the object indicates that it is not the good and bad object that are being kept apart but an idealized and extremely bad one. So deep and sharp a division reveals that destructive impulses, envy, and persecutory anxiety are very strong and that idealization serves mainly as a defense against these emotions . . . excessive idealization denotes that persecution is the main driving force. (pp. 24–25)

This idea, that splitting characterized by ideal objects typically denotes a defense against persecutory anxiety rather than a relationship with a good object per se, becomes a critical distinction between her work and Kohut's—but it anticipates the work of Kernberg. In the next chapter, we will discuss the contributions of both.

This short summary of Klein's late assumptions about splitting indicates its continuing importance. But it predates her concept of the depressive position and the manic defenses, which while developmentally later, predate the paranoid-schizoid position and the importance she later attached to envy. To grasp this progression one must return to her early work.

EARLY CONTRIBUTIONS

Klein began her work with children while in Budapest in 1919, with the encouragement of Sandor Ferenczi. She read her first paper to the Budapest Psychoanalytic Society in July, 1919, and an expanded version was published in 1921. In this paper, "Development of a Child," Klein suggests the splitting-off of a female imago in the case of her young male patient, the result of an untenable ambivalent attitude toward females. A phantasy of a witch "introduces a figure . . . that he had, it seems to me, obtained by division of the mother-imago. I see this too in the occasionally ambivalent attitude toward the female sex . . . recently become evident in him." (p. 42) Untenable ambivalence regressed to splitting—one imago with a penis, and the other without.

By 1929, Klein had already suggested an earlier genesis of the oedipal conflict than Freud supposed, and had unexpectedly discovered a cruel superego, made up of multiple identifications, in the very young child. In "Personification in the Play of Children" (1929), she states:

> The necessity for a synthesis of the super-ego arises out of the difficulty experienced by the subject in coming to an understanding of the super-ego made up of imagos of such opposite natures. . . .
>
> I have come to the conclusion that the splitting of the super-ego into the primal identifications introjected at different stages of development is a mechanism analogous to and closely connected with projection. I believe these mechanisms (splitting-up and projection) are a principal factor in the tendency to personification in play. By their means the synthesis of the super-ego, which can be maintained only with more or less effort, can be given up for the time being and, further, the tension of maintaining the truce between the super-ego as a whole and the id is diminished. The intrapsychic conflict becomes less violent and can be displaced into the external world. (p. 221)

Klein seems to be accounting here for the splitting of objects in the childhood psyche. At this point in her psychoanalytic conceptualization she is positing that objects are incorporated throughout the various phases of libidinal development and at first are incompatible and inconsistent with each other and therefore appear to be split. A necessity for a synthesis for these disparate imagos takes place in order to achieve harmony in the superego. Noteworthy, however, is her linking up splitting with projection, denoting their mutual interaction. Later in the same paper she states:

> We see then that a weakening of the conflict or its displacement into the external world by means of the mechanisms of *splitting up and projection* is one of the principal incentives to transference and a driving force in analytic work. . . . In schizophrenia, in my opinion, the capacity for personification and for transference fails, amongst other reasons, through the defective functioning of the projection mechanism (and defensive splitting). (p.224; my italics)

In this passage Klein is again linking splitting and projection as two interlocking defense mechanisms which help the infantile psyche to defend against unwanted feelings, but, in addition, she also considers the capacity to develop transference and its dependency on splitting and projection, which she later is to call projective identification. Notice also her allusion to *defective* splitting and projection in psychosis.

THE DEPRESSIVE POSITION

"A Contribution to the Psychogenesis of Manic-Depressive States" (1935) represents Klein's first systematic account of concepts she had developed earlier, while she on one hand accepted classical Freudian psychosexual development, but on the other hand had utilized different terminology for her original approach to child analysis. Now she depended on the theory of the life and death instincts, interacting through the expressions of love and hate, articulated via a new view of the origin of manic-depressive illness. She states:

Among the various internal demands which go to make up the severity of the super-ego in the melancholic, I have mentioned his urgent need to comply with the very strict demands of the 'good' objects. It is this part of the picture only—namely, the cruelty of the 'good', *i.e.* loved, objects within—which has been recognized by general analytic opinion; it became clear in the relentless severity of the super- ego of the melancholic. But in my view it is only by looking at the whole relation of the ego to its phantastically bad objects as well as to its good objects, only by looking at the whole picture of the internal situation . . . that we can understand the slavery to which the ego submits when complying with the externally cruel demands and admonitions of its loved object which has become installed within the ego. As I have mentioned before, *the ego endeavors to keep the good apart from the bad, and the real from the phantastic objects.* [My italics.] The result is a conception of extremely bad and *extremely perfect* objects, that is to say, its loved objects are in many ways intensely more unexacting. At the same time, as the infant cannot fully keep his good and bad objects apart in his mind, some of the cruelty of the bad objects and of the id becomes attached to the good objects and this then again increases the severity of their demands. (pp. 288-289)

Here for the first time Melanie Klein is talking about her now famous split between good and bad internal objects which are formed by the projective identification of loving and hostile feelings from the infant. Not only must these objects be kept apart in the ego; they must also be kept apart in the superego. At the earliest stage of development there tends to be an absolute polarization of attitudes toward these objects; in other words, they are either all good or all bad.

No doubt, the more the child can at this stage develop a happy relationship to its real mother, the more it will be able to overcome the depressive position. But all depends on how it is able to find its way out of the conflict between love and uncontrollable hatred and sadism. As I have pointed out before, in the earliest phase the persecuting and the good objects are kept wide apart in the child's mind. When, along with the introjection of

> the whole and real object, they come closer together, the ego has over and over again recourse to that mechanism—so important for the development of the relations to objects—namely, a splitting of its imagos into loved and hated, that is to say, into good and dangerous ones. (p. 308)

Klein also delineates in this paper her important distinction between splitting and ambivalence. She points out that the classical use of the latter term tends to be confused with what one might more properly call splitting of objects and egos. In other words, the anxieties of the depressive position, which comes about when the infant forms a unified conception of mother, are characterized by the unification of incompatible attitudes toward the goodness and badness of objects. Before the depressive position, a good object is not in any way the same thing as a bad object. It is only in the depressive position that polar qualities can be seen as different aspects of the same object. It was also in this paper that Melanie Klein first offered the concept of the *infantile depressive position.*

> One might think that it is actually at this point that *ambivalence,* which, after all, refers to object-relations—that is to say, to whole and real objects—sets in. Ambivalence, carried out in the splitting of the imagos, enables the young child to gain more trust and belief in its real objects and thus in its internalized ones—to love them more and to carry out in an increasing degree its phantasies of restoration of the loved object. . . .
>
> It seems that at this stage of development the unification of external and internal, loved and hated, real and imaginary objects is carried out in such a way that each step in the unification leads again to a renewed splitting of the imagos. But, as the adaptation to the external world increases, this splitting is carried out on planes which gradually become increasingly nearer and nearer to reality. This goes on until love for the real and the internalized objects and trust in them are well established. (pp. 308–309)

The ambivalence that we commonly see in obsessive-compulsive neurosis, for instance, is less ambivalence than it is alternating splitting of epiphanies of a good and bad object, each disconnected or split off from the other. To Klein, ambivalence is the simultaneous existence of two incompatible attitudes within the state of consciousness about an identical object. Another way of stating this is to say that ambivalence predicates the third dimension of the depth perception of an object, in which people are not omnipotent or "on stage" as characters in a family romance or a fairy tale.

Klein's 1940 paper, "Mourning and Its Relation to Manic-Depressive States," is an extension of her 1935 contribution, and it solidifies her concept of the depressive position. She shows that the ability to mourn relies on the resolution of that position in childhood, and demonstrates the importance of more realistic splitting to prevail in order to allow for mourning rather than a manic-depressive condition.

> There is a constant interaction between anxieties relating to the 'external' mother—as I will call her in contrast to the 'internal' one—and those relating to the 'internal' mother, and the methods used by the ego for dealing with these two sets of anxieties are closely inter-related. In the baby's mind the 'internal' mother is bound up with the 'external' one of whom she is a 'double,' though one which once undergoes alterations in his mind through the very process of internalization; that is to say, her image is influenced by his phantasies, and by internal stimuli and internal experiences of all kinds. When external situations which he lives through become internalized—and I hold that they do, from the earliest days onwards—they follow the same pattern: they also become 'doubles' of real situations, and are again altered for the same reasons. The fact that by being internalized, people, things, situations and happenings—the whole inner world which is being built up—become inaccessible to the child's accurate observation and judgment, and cannot be verified by the means of perception which are available in connection with the tangible and palpable object-world, has an important bearing on the phantastic nature of this inner world. ... The visible mother thus provides continuous proofs of what the 'internal' mother is like, whether she is loving or angry, helpful or revengeful. The extent to which external reality is able

to disprove anxieties and sorrow relating to the internal reality varies with each individual, but could be taken as one of the criteria for normality. (p. 313)

In this pivotal contribution Klein extends not only the importance of the distinction between the good breast and the bad breast (good and bad objects), but also definitively delineates the distinction via splitting between the internal world and the external world and discusses the relationship between each. She also has established the depressive position as the beginning of the infantile neurosis.

The resolution of splitting of selves and objects in the depressive position occurs through what Klein calls *reparation*. The infant becomes, as development proceeds, inescapably aware of the separation from the object (the primal split) and simultaneously becomes aware of guilt toward the object in regard to phantasied damage done to it. Probably the infant's speculation about why mother split him off stimulates his awareness of this guilt. As the infant longs for the departing mother, he also is restoring her as an image of representation in his mind. This process requires surrendering or releasing the possessively held internal objects (which are split) and allowing for the awareness of mother's absence without omnipotent possessiveness. The adoption of the whole object also allows the split between the ego proper and the ego invested in the object to come together. Splitting is then no longer necessary as a primitive defense; it proceeds through neutralization and sublimation to a change of function. Its more mature form is repression, and it also facilitates, as an ego apparatus, discrimination and differentiation, perceptually and cognitively.

THE PARANOID-SCHIZOID POSITION

"Notes on Some Schizoid Mechanisms" (1946) is the final paper in the important theoretical triumvirate that articulated the early months of life based on the life and death instincts.

(The other two papers, discussed above, are "A Contribution to the Psychogenesis of Manic-Depressive States" and "Mourning and Its Relation to Manic-Depressive States.") In this paper, Klein formally discusses the importance of splitting in infantile development as a *schizoid* technique which (along with the mechanisms of projective identification, magic omnipotent denial, and idealization) determines the formation of early psychic life. She calls the earliest cosmos of mental life the paranoid position (later, following Fairbairn, the paranoid-schizoid position) because of the persecutory nature of the internal objects created by projective identification. A split-off object or element of self in this position could be denied by being projected into another object; projective identification, Klein thought, continued the work of splitting.

Implicit in Klein's assumptions about the split and persecutory cosmos is the difficulty that the infant has in maintaining a single focus, so to speak, on his external and internal world. The advent of the depressive position will permit consolidation, but, "At this time," writes Klein in "On the Theory of Anxiety and Guilt" (1952a),

> that is, during the first three to four months of life, splitting processes, involving the splitting of the first object (the breast) as well as of the feelings towards it, are at their height. Hatred and persecutory anxiety become attached to the frustrating (bad) breast, and love and reassurance to the gratifying (good) breast. However, even at this stage such splitting processes are never fully effective; for from the beginning of life the ego tends towards integrating itself and towards synthesizing the different aspects of the object. (This tendency can be regarded as an expression of the Life Instinct.) (pp. 282–283)

Klein seems to imply here that splitting works dialectically to achieve some kind of optimum equilibrium that will allow for integration without catastrophe. As such, she explicates splitting as an important element in the growth of the human psyche—a fundamental basis for what I have termed the *princi-*

ple of distinction, by which I mean that splitting underlies discriminatory processes as well as defensive processes antecedent to projective identification.

There are also different intensities to splitting. In "Some Theoretical Conclusions Regarding the Emotional Life of the Infant" (1952b), Klein states:

> there are great variations in the strength, frequency, and duration of splitting processes (not only between individuals but also in the same infant at different times) . . . for instance, it appears that together with splitting the breast into two aspects, loved and hated (good and bad), splitting of a different nature exists which gives rise to the feeling that the ego, as well as its object, is in pieces; these processes underlie states of disintegration. . . . The early methods of splitting fundamentally influence the ways in which, at a somewhat later stage, repression is carried out and this in turn determines the degree of interaction between conscious and unconscious. In other words, the extent to which the various parts of the mind remain 'porous' in relation to one another is determined largely by the strength or weakness of the early schizoid mechanisms. (p. 204)

"Porous splitting" is less rigid and permits the development of a later repression, and the factor determining this seems to be the strength or weakness of the early schizoid mechanisms—particularly of splitting itself.

> There is also a difference in the use of splitting the object and the self. The ego, although earlier methods of splitting continue in some degree, now divides the complete object into an uninjured live object and an injured and endangered one (perhaps dying or dead); splitting thus becomes largely a defense against depressive anxiety. (p. 213)

After its inception in the paranoid-schizoid position where it deals with early part-objects, splitting begins to divide whole objects—such as live object and dead object—anticipatory to the whole object relationships which occur at the threshold of the depressive position.

Finally,

> The mechanism of splitting underlies repression . . . but in contrast to the earliest forms of splitting which lead to states of disintegration, repression does not normally result in the disintegration of the self. Since at this stage there is greater integration, both within the conscious and the unconscious parts of the mind, and since in repression the splitting predominantly effects a division between conscious and unconscious, neither part of the self is exposed to the degree of disintegration which may arise in previous stages. However, the extent to which splitting processes are resorted to in the first few months of life vitally influences the use of repression at a later stage. For if the early schizoid mechanisms and anxieties have not been sufficiently overcome, the result may be that instead of a fluid boundary between the conscious and the unconscious a rigid barrier arises; this indicates that repression is excessive in that, in consequence, development is disturbed. . . . This capacity is linked with the greater synthesis within the super-ego and the growing assimilation of the super-ego by the ego. (pp. 228–229)

The development of repression itself is predicated on the graduation of splitting, that is, of its normal development alongside the diminution of omnipotence. And if splitting is able to establish a fluid boundary between the conscious and the unconscious, then normal repression and superego development can occur.

4

Other Contributions

Besides Freud, other early analysts contributed to the literature on splitting, notably Sandor Ferenczi and Otto Rank. A number of remarks appear in Ferenczi's posthumous notes and fragments, and "Each Adaptation is Preceded by an Inhibited Attempt at Splitting" (1930), which discusses the essential nature of the process, is especially interesting. Rank's 1914 monograph, *The Double*, shows that more than any analyst before or since, he is aware of the importance of this phenomenon in continental, English, and American literature, and he traces its impact on Freud's thinking. His views correspond closely to my own clinical perspective on splitting insofar as he emphasizes the splitting of personalities rather than of instincts and instinct derivatives.

Melanie Klein's influence has been central, however, for contributions on splitting, and in this chapter we will focus briefly on four of her followers, and then on three important steps made by analysts more closely associated with classical thought.

It is to Fairbairn that modern psychoanalysis and psychiatry owe so much for his formulations of the schizoid personality and his emphasis on splitting. Winnicott's concept of the true and false selves has been of major importance, and adumbrates Kohut's conceptions of the idealized and mirroring transferences in narcissistic disorders. Of all Klein's followers,

Rosenfeld has perhaps made the most extensive attempts to clarify the nature of normal and abnormal splitting. Finally, Bion was perhaps the first psychoanalyst to call attention to macroscopic splits in the borderline personalities and in psychotics; his important work, "Attacks on Linking" (1959a), will be discussed at length in chapter 11.

Although classical authors have not always completely acknowledged indebtedness to Klein and her followers, their important influence has been clear. Kernberg has introduced the ideas of Klein and Fairbairn into classical theory with notable success. Certain aspects of Kohut's thinking are also related to Kleinian ideas. Finally, Mahler, who had early on accepted Klein's description of early defense mechanisms, has found evidence of splitting in her studies of normal infants and children.

W. R. D. FAIRBAIRN

Fairbairn explicitly stated what the classical structural theory loosely implied: the personality is divided or split into subgroupings and that these subgroupings or splits are functional autonomies within the personality. This was the first step away from the classical notion of motivation in the personality as due solely to the stochastic bombardment of the ego by instinctual impulses. The id was no longer a separate structure but was part of an ego complex. This was the forerunner of the concept of the intersystemic suborganization (Lichtenberg and Slap 1973) and also adumbrated Kernberg's structural theory of object relations. Fairbairn believed that splitting is the prime phenomenon which confronts the personality, pathologically speaking, and the task of growth and of psychoanalysis is to unite the splits. He was able to correlate the splittings of the ego with splittings of objects in identificatory relationships to the egos. His emphasis on splitting so appealed to Melanie Klein that she renamed the paranoid position the paranoid-schizoid position.

Fairbairn (1952) conceived of a separate ego from birth,

emerging from a state of primary identification. Traumata perforate the pristine unity of primary identification into splits of egos and objects. The principal residue of this abruption of primary identification is *(a)* a *central ego* relating to an ideal object, the two comprising an endopsychic structure which represses *(b)* an *antilibidinal ego* identified with a rejecting object as a second endopsychic structure which, in turn, represses *(c)* a third endopsychic structure composed of a *libidinal ego* and an exciting object.

The antilibidinal ego and the rejecting object comprise a primitive, talion superego, whereas the ideal object, in association with the central ego, is more of a moral superego. The central ego and the idealized object repress both these endopsychic structures, and, in turn, the libidinal ego as exciting or needed objects are repressed by the antilibidinal and rejecting object. This triumvirate of structures is but one configuration which can take place in the psyche in terms of traumatic cleavages.

The ego for Fairbairn is essentially schizoid because it is comprised of splits, normally and pathologically. The process of development and maturation is to bring these splits together into a cohesive unit.

The schizoid individual, on the other hand, denotes that personality type which is characterized by marked splitting off of awareness and the development of a noninsightful introspection which results in a rich fantasy life, a split-off reality, and a disposition characterized by inner omnipotence and omniscience in contrast to feelings of inferiority and impotence vis-à-vis the external world.

Fairbairn's endopsychic structures are dynamic structures which are combinations of egos and instinctual drives. It was his belief that instincts, like all psychic energy, cannot be separated from structure. Kernberg's later object relations theory owes a great deal in its structual form to Fairbairn's concepts, not to mention its debt to the work of Melanie Klein. Kohut, on the other hand, owes his new instinct theory almost solely to Fairbairn.

As a consequence of his concept of the primacy of splitting and the installation of endopsychic structures along the fault lines of these splits, Fairbairn further conceived that maturation and development of the personality occur in proportion as the splits come together. Whereas the period of primal splitting occupies the schizoid position and the depressive position, Fairbairn envisioned a transitional phase in which neurotic techniques of relating to the object supplant psychotic techniques. These neurotic techniques are as follows:

1. *Obsessional:* in which there is alternation between trying to evacuate a bad object and retain a good object. Since the bad object is the content (feces), however, indecision reigns so that both objects are retained.

2. *Phobic:* in which the bad object is evacuated and distanced, but the good object is also easily lost since it is stationary, will not move, and, furthermore, causes claustrophobic anxiety—so it also must be evacuated.

3. *Hysterical:* in which the bad object is retained and identified with, whereas the good object is projected into an idealized object for safekeeping.

4. *Paranoid:* in which the good object is internalized and the bad object is projected outside.

In the final stage, mature dependency, the transitional neurotic techniques of dealing with psychotic splits yield to an ambivalent state in which the split egos and objects come together in a recognition of the central importance of mutual dependency.

D. W. WINNICOTT

Discussing the impulse or expectation of the infant and impinging reality as two "lines," Winnicott (1948) asks:

> What are the consequences of failure in the introduction of the shared world to the infant? In the extreme of failure these two lines in a diagram would be parallel. The infant creates out of his native poverty, and the world impinges in vain. The lines never meet. In such a hypothetical case there must be mental defect

even if there is normal brain capacity. Commonly there is some degree of this splitting at the earliest level, and the basis thereby laid for the infant to have a relationship unshared by us with a self-created world in which magic holds sway, and alongside this a compliance with mundane management from outside, convenient because life-giving, but unsatisfactory in the extreme to the infant. Later on in childhood or adult life the compliance breaks down, if it is too isolated from the other trend which contains all the child's spontaneity. These parallel paths regularly appear in our analytic work, illustrated at the simplest by the patient who said that his analytic sessions were in duplicate, a rather dull one actually with the analyst, and the operative one afterwards in relation to an imagined analyst. (p. 170)

In the best of situations a split seems to take place between phantasy and reality. Winnicott, like Fairbairn, believed that with disappointment in early environmental relationships, particularly with a key object like the mother, the infant might withdraw his true feeling self into an inner, isolated state, leaving his denuded, disenfranchised self on the outside to conform as best it could with the demands of the external world.

Winnicott's concept of the "true" and the "false" selves was a major contribution to the theory of splitting and adumbrated Kohut's conceptions of the idealized and mirroring transferences in narcissistic disorders. Winnicott believed that the infant who is subjected to mothering which is not "good enough" may experience a split in his personality in which a factotum or disembodied self (false self) carries on as usual in the external world, having been deserted by its true self which is experienced as having withdrawn into the inner recesses of the ego (Winnicott 1952, 1960). The true self hopes to enter seclusion so as to "heal." Insofar as the false self is in contact with a hostile environment, it becomes progressively demoralized by a need to conform to the overwhelming pressures.

In "Aggression in Relation to Emotional Development" (1950) he states:

In my description there now comes a place for anger at frustration. Frustration, which is inevitable in some degree in all experience, encourages the dichotomy: 1. innocent agressive impulses towards frustrating objects, and 2. guilt-productive aggressive impulses towards good objects. Frustration acts as a seduction away from guilt and fosters a defence mechanism, namely, the direction of love and hate along separate lines. If this splitting of objects into good and bad takes place, there is an easing of guilt feeling; but in payment the love loses some of its valuable aggressive component, and the hate becomes the more disruptive. (p. 207)

In other words frustration mitigates guilt feelings and encourages what Melanie Klein called a manic defense against the emergence of guilt by superimposing upon the object which would inspire it. The cleavage lines between frustration and guilt are confused by anger and since the good object, towards whom we feel guilt feelings when we are angry, becomes felt to be an obstructing object, the anger at the obstructing object only confuses and eclipses the guilt feelings toward the originally good object.

HERBERT ROSENFELD

Rosenfeld, following Klein, makes the distinction between normal and abnormal splitting mechanisms. In the former category, he includes developmental splitting, characteristic for the paranoid-schizoid position, in which the infant has the task of differentiating or splitting between his loving and hateful impulses. He must also differentiate between the objects of these impulses, the good and bad breast or good and bad objects. Normal splitting extends into the differentiation between zones of the body such as the mouth, anus, and genitals, and of the zones of the body of the object; distinctions must also be made between psychological and geographic qualities such as internal and external, meaningful and irrelevant, etc. Ultimately, according to Rosenfeld, splitting becomes sublimated (or neutralized), as the capacity for repression, and on the other as the capacity for cognitive discrimination and differentiation.

Abnormal splitting is characterized by excessive splitting, splintering, and fragmentation. In these cases, the excessive nature of the splitting is aided by increased destructiveness and by abnormal projective identification. In "Remarks on the Relation of Male Homosexuality to Paranoia, Paranoid Anxiety and Narcissism" (1949), Rosenfeld states the example of a dream of a patient in which a German professor on a motorcycle tried to split himself in two by running against a gatepost. In his dream, the splitting was increased by the fact that the patient felt himself so confused with the analyst.

Rosenfeld (1950) discusses acute confusional states "in which love and hate impulses and good and bad objects cannot be kept apart and are thus felt to be mixed up or confused. These infantile states of confusion are states of disintegration and are related to the *confusional schizophrenic states of the adult*" (p. 53). Without normal differentiation, according to Rosenfeld, splitting mechanisms are reinforced, and in analysis one frequently realizes that the various split-off parts of the ego are identified with introjected good or bad objects. He sees two ways in which the confusional states are overcome. First, the ego may regain the power of differentiation between the libidinal and the aggressive impulses. The result is better integration and clinical improvement. Secondly, the normal differentiation between aggressive and libidinal impulses fails, subsequently *new splitting mechanisms* make their appearance, *or the existing tendencies to split become reinforced.* "After the splitting becomes activated, the confusion and anxiety disappears, but there is clinically a deterioration in the patient's state, since the splitting causes progressive disintegration of the ego. An acute confusional state is apt to occur when splitting processes lessen, either spontaneously or through analysis, and both libidinal and aggressive impulses may temporarily predominate and interfere with the attempt at recovery." (p. 61)

Thus, Rosenfeld is extending Klein's conception of splitting between good and bad objects to the differentiation between the actions of the libidinal instinct and the death instinct. If a normal distinction (normal splitting) between them fails, then the new splitting mechanisms which substitute for the defective ones become highly destructive and highly polarized. Defensive splitting is thought by Klein and her followers to be one of the vicissitudes of the death instinct in the first place and is therefore used paradoxically to conduct a splitting between the libidinal and the destructive instincts. This secondary or abnormal splitting is highly polarized and results in abnormal splitting with an ego defect. This concept as brought forth in this paper seems to be the progenitor of Kernberg's (1975) conceptualization of polarized splitting in the borderline personality.

Hypochondriasis and psychosomatic diseases, according to Rosenfeld, also represent confusional anxieties which

> are split-off into the body, a process which probably starts in early infancy, but becomes reinforced during later development. Further splitting processes go on simultaneously. Early oral sadistic, omnipotent impulses, particularly envy, also seem unbearable to the early ego, which gives rise to splitting. In hypochondriasis, the oral sadism and its later derivatives are partly split-off, and the part which is split-off seems to be projected by the ego into external objects and quickly introjected into the body and body organs. (p. 187)

It must be remembered that Kleinian formulations belong to that inchoate state of infant development in which the infant experiences itself as a *body ego* and, conversely, objects as bodily objects. As a result, the splitting off of painful states of mind are thought of as splitting off painful aspects of a body self which are then projectively identified in interpersonal body objects, and then the amalgam is introjected as a split-off confused body self-object. In other words, the introject includes the split-off and projected aspects of the original ego's body self which is now contained inside as a confused amalgam of the split-off self and the interpersonal object.

Rosenfeld (1964) finds that acting-out in psychotic states has the effect of trying to polarize the goodness and the badness of the objects so as to create a split in lieu of the one that is not there. It polarizes the external environment into being either persecutory or definitive in its relationships to the patient, and it serves, therefore, as a solid boundary of unambiguity for him or her to confront. This lessens psychotic confusion. Acting-out in depressives and neurotics, on the other hand, has an entirely different mechanism; in neurotics its purpose is to increase the splitting between the self and its awareness of its own depressive feelings.

WILFRED BION

Bion first called attention to macroscopic splits in borderline and psychotic patients in his paper, "The Imaginary Twin," published in 1950. He discusses the phantasies of three patients who created twins to use for projections; in each case there were prominent associations to disturbances of vision. Bion wondered whether "the psychological development was bound up with the development of ocular control in the same way that problems of development linked with oral aggression co-exist with the eruption of teeth." (p. 22) This early physiological development was in turn related to oedipal phantasies. The infant may create an imaginary twin of himself in association with a splitting of the parental couple by creating a failure of binocular fusion due to the mechanism of conversion. Bion's concept spans the gulf from early neurophysiological differentiations and interpretations (a splitting of the senses), through the normal childhood tendency to construct an imaginary companion (a phenomenon which ordinarily goes into repression) and its pathological reemergence in later life.

Referring to Klein's discussion of symbol formation, Bion asks: "Is it possible that the capacity to personify splittings of the personality is in some way analogous to a capacity for symbol formation. . . ?" (p. 20). He suggests that, in the patient he had observed, regressions had taken place away from any increase in capacity for psychological development, resulting in a unique splitting between two partially developed portions of the personality which had sufficient rudimentary elements of symbol formation to allow separate status.

In "Notes on the Theory of Schizophrenia" (1953), Bion states that schizophrenic language is used as a mode of action which serves the splitting of the object or projective identification. It is the use of words as things or as split-off parts of oneself which the patient pushes forcefully into the analyst and is employed as a mode of action for the splitting of his object. The patient's language conveys that double-bind or "Catch-22" enigma in which any answer is attacked by another aspect of the question. Schizophrenic language, that is, is split and also splits the conceptual receptions of the receiver. Bion thinks this aspect of schizophrenic language has the purpose of splitting the analyst, "who is not allowed to go to sleep and is not allowed to keep awake." (p. 25)

> The severe splitting in the schizophrenic makes it difficult for him to achieve the use of symbols and subsequently of substantives and verbs. . . . The capacity to form symbols is dependent on:
> (1) The ability to grasp the whole objects.
> (2) The abandonment of the paranoid-schizoid position with its attendant splitting.
> (3) The bringing together of splits and the ushering in of the depressive position. (p. 26)

In other words, because of the schizophrenic's hatred of his embryonic capacity for verbal thought he splits off his capacity to relate to or grasp whole objects, adheres tenaciously and fixatedly to the paranod-schizoid position, and maintains the splits between self and objects, self and selves, and objects and objects. The coming together of these splits would spell that quintessential doom known as significance, which is the main experience of the depressive position. Schizophrenic patients believe that splitting has destroyed their capacity to think.

In his paper "Differentiation of the Psychotic from the Non-Psychotic Personalities" (1957a) Bion states,

I wish to emphasize that in this phase the psychotic splits his objects, and contemporaneously all that part of his personality, which would make him aware of the reality he hates, into exceedingly minute fragments, for it is this that contributes materially to the psychotic's feelings that he cannot restore his objects or his ego. As a result of these splitting attacks, all those features of the personality which should one day provide the foundation for intuitive understanding of himself and others are jeopardized at the outset. (p. 47)

Primitive thought is attacked because it links sense impressions with consciousness, but also,

thanks to the psychotic's over endowment with destructiveness, the splitting processes are extended to the links within the thought processes themselves. . . . All these now are attacked till finally two objects cannot be brought together in a way which leaves each object with its intrinsic qualities intact and yet able, by their conjunction, to produce a new mental object. Consequently the formation of symbols, which depends for its therapeutic effect on the ability to bring together two objects so that the resemblance is made manifest, yet their difference left unimpaired, now becomes difficult. At a still later stage the result of these splitting attacks is seen in the denial of articulation as a principle for the combining of words. . . . Further, since that-which-links has been not only minutely fragmented but also projected out into objects to join the other bizarre objects, the patient feels surrounded by minute links which, being impregnated now with cruelty, link objects together cruelly. (p. 50)

Bion is discussing macroscopic splits between the psychotic and nonpsychotic parts of the personality, and he believes that the former is the result of an infantile mental catastrophe due to the perception by the infant of a mother whose "reverie" was insufficient to contain his projections. (*Reverie* is Bion's term for the capacity of the mother to so contain the infant's projections, to be able to dilute them, sort them, decipher them, and convert them into appropriate action or forbearance.) The mother is therefore believed to have been *(a)* destroyed, and *(b)* transformed into an obstructive internal object which refuses to contain projections. (Bion 1957b, 1959a)

In "On Hallucination" (1958) Bion makes a clear-cut distinction between what might be called a molar, or whole object, dissociative quality and the minute splitting or fragmentation characteristic of the paranoid-schizoid position, especially when hypertrophied in psychotic conditions. Dissociative phenomena which occur along clean lines are more characteristic of hysterical states. "It seems to me," he writes,

> that the phenomena which I have observed in this and other severely disturbed patients are best described by the term "splitting" as it is used by Melanie Klein, leaving the term "dissociation" free to be employed where a more benign activity is being discussed. The original splitting processes evinced by this patient were violent, intended to produce minute fragmentation and deliberately aimed at effecting separations which run directly counter to any natural lines of demarcation between one part of the psyche, or one function of the psyche, and another. Dissociation on the other hand appears to be gentler and to have respect for natural lines of demarcation between whole objects and indeed to follow those lines of demarcation to effect the separation; the patient who dissociates is capable of depression. Dissociation also appears to me to betray dependence on the pre-existence of elementary verbal thought, as indeed Freud's statement that "it is the common popular idea of the organs and of the body in general that it is at work in the hysterical paralyses" would seem to indicate. (p. 69)

In all of the papers discussed above, which were republished in his *Second Thoughts* (1967), Bion emphasizes the development or ontogeny of splitting from its primitive and inchoate roots to its more sophisticated expression as a dissociative phenomenon in the depressive position. He is mainly interested in its effect in schizophrenia on attacking the links in communication and conceptualization (see chapter 7, this volume). In another contribution, *Learning From Experience* (1962b), Bion suggests that in addition to the type of splitting described by Klein (between the life and death instincts and the good and bad objects), there is yet another, more subtle, type of splitting which operates on the difference between the *needed,* as opposed to the *desired,* aspects of the object. The infant may, because of enormous envious hatred of his needed object, compromise by remaining aware of his need but split off the desirability of the object onto material possessions which are more under the power of the person to obtain for himself and which are divested of human qualities. Materialism, therefore, contains the desirability, and the human object is the repository of need. The resultant personality is split in loyalties, indecisive and schizoid in temperament, and seems to be condemned to remain that way for the rest of his life.

HEINZ KOHUT

In *The Analysis of the Self* (1971), Kohut states:

> The acceptance by the analyst of the phase-appropriateness of the analysand's narcissistic demands counteracts the chronic tendency of the reality ego to wall itself off from the unrealistic narcissistic structures by such mechanisms as repression, isolation, or disavowal. Correlated to the last-named mechanism is a specific, chronic structural change to which I would like to refer, in a modification of Freud's terminology. . . . as a *vertical split in the psyche.* The ideational and emotional manifestations of a vertical split in the psyche—in contrast to such *horizontal splits* as those brought about on a deeper level by repression and on a higher level by negation . . . —are correlated to the side by side, conscious existence of otherwise incompatible psychological attitudes *in depth.* (pp. 176–177)

Thus, Kohut distinguishes between two groups of narcissistic personality techniques of splitting. In the first, the archaic grandiose self exists in a repressed or in a negated state. This, according to Kohut, comprises a horizontal split in the psyche and therefore deprives the reality ego of the narcissistic enrichment of narcissistic energy. The result will be symptoms of a narcissistic deficiency characterized by diminished self-confidence, vague depression, absence of zest for work, and lack of initiative.

In the second group there is the presence of an unmodified grandiose self which is separated from the reality orientation of the psyche via a vertical split. Here the grandiose self is conscious and therefore casts a strong influence on many activities of the personality. Such individuals may act, therefore, narcissistically in the general sense of the word by being impetuous, peremptory, and self-assertive in the extreme. They also seem to contain a silently repressed grandiose self on the lines of the aforementioned horizontal split, with symptoms much as previously discussed. These patients will therefore be more likely to vacillate between extremes of grandiosity and self-deprecation.

Kohut has also emphasized an important new concept in psychoanalysis, which I believe (Grotstein 1978, 1980e) to be best described as a *dual track*. He envisions a separate agenda for the development of the self on one hand, and the development of the self's relations to objects on the other. This concept of separate agendas for the self and its relationships is suggestive of a normal dissociation within the self.

OTTO KERNBERG

Kernberg has successfully introduced ideas drawn from Melanie Klein and from Fairbairn into classical analytic thought. His emphasis on the importance of early states of the mind borrows heavily from Klein in a dynamic sense, and from Fairbairn in a structural sense. His theoretical orientation emphasizes splitting and its effects on early object structuralization.

In his 1975 treatment of the borderline personality organization, Kernberg states: "Introjections and identifications established under the influence of libidinal drive derivatives are at first built up separately from those established under the influence of aggressive drive derivatives ('good' and 'bad' internal objects, or 'positive' and 'negative' introjections)" (p. 25). Later Kernberg altered this formulation to stress the distinction in the affective experience of pleasure and unpleasure, in which each affect was to orchestrate subsequent self-object representations. But in either case, this

> division of internal object relations into "good" and "bad" happens at first simply because of the lack of integrative capacity of the early ego. Later on, what originally was a lack of integrative capacity is used defensively by the emerging ego in order to prevent the generalization of anxiety and to protect the ego core built around positive introjections (introjections and identifications established under the influence of libidinal drive derivatives). *This defensive division of the ego, in which what was at first a simple defect in integration is then used actively for other purposes, is in essence the mechanism of splitting.* This mechanism is normally used only in an early stage of ego development during the first year of life, and rapidly is replaced by higher level defensive operations of the ego which center around repression and related mechanisms such as reaction formation, isolation, and undoing, all of which protect the ego from intrapsychic conflicts by means of the rejection of a drive derivative or its ideational representation, or both, from the conscious ego. In contrast, in pathological conditions when this mechanism. . . . persists, splitting protects the ego from conflicts by means of the dissociation or active maintaining apart of introjections and identifications of strongly conflictual nature, namely, those libidinally determined from those aggressively determined, without regard to the access to consciousness. (pp. 25–26)

In other words, Kernberg believes splitting to be a basic mechanism which passively influences the formation of distinctions between good and bad self-object representations. Later, after considerable growth and development, regressive elaborations involve much more forceful and active splitting mechanisms. Kernberg furthermore believes splitting to be an important underlying mechanism in the formation of the borderline personality. He uses splitting in a restricted sense to refer to the active process of keeping apart introjections and identifications of opposite quality. His insistence on this restriction is a way of differentiating his views from those of Klein and

Fairbairn. Splitting, he believes, is a fundamental cause of ego weakness and, since it requires less countercathectic energy than does repression, a weak ego becomes all the more easily victimized, creating a vicious circle in which ego weakness and splitting reinforce each other.

Splitting may be manifested, according to Kernberg, as an alternation between clinical symptoms where contradictions are manifest and yet denied. Splitting may also be evident by selective lack of impulse control, addictions, and abrupt shifts of identifications between "all good" and "all bad" objects. Kernberg believes splitting to occur in "extreme and repetitive oscillation between contradictory and self concepts. . . ." He also states that splitting is a characteristic feature in primitive idealization, early forms of projection and projective identification, denial, and omnipotence and devaluation—all of which correspond to Melanie Klein's so-called "schizoid mechanisms."

In his later work on object relations, Kernberg (1976) continued his delineation of splitting without further conceptualization.

MARGARET MAHLER

Mahler acknowledged the importance of Klein's description of primitive defense mechanisms in her early papers dealing with childhood psychosis (Mahler and Gosliner 1955). In her pioneering work descriptive of the development of normal infants and children (Mahler, Pine, and Bergman 1975), she sees splitting as an important mechanism albeit one that does not make its appearance until the beginning of the symbiotic subphase where the differentiation of pleasurable and unpleasurable qualities seems to be its "quasi-ontogenetic basis." Splitting as it later appears is generally characterized by absolute splitting between good and bad qualities of the object, identified with the self-representations split in accordance. Mahler believes furthermore that such splits can become foci of permanent islands of developmental failures leading to borderline phenomena. In the glossary splitting is defined as a defense mechanism often found during the rapprochement subphase (once a certain measure of ego development has been achieved); the toddler cannot easily tolerate simultaneous love and hate feelings toward the same person. Love and hate are not amalgamated; mother is experienced alternately as all good or all bad. Another possibility is that the absent mother is felt to be all good while others become all bad. Hence the toddler may displace aggression onto the nonmother world while exaggerating love for (overidealizing) the absent, longed-for mother. When mother returns she disrupts the ideal image, and reunions with her are often painful, since the young ego's synthetic function cannot heal the split. In most cases gradual synthesis of all "good" and all "bad" by the growing ego becomes possible. (pp. 292–293)

Rapprochement is the third subphase of separation-individuation (which is described as occurring from sixteen or eighteen to twenty-four months and beyond), and

in those children with less than optimal development, the ambivalence conflict is discernible during the rapprochement subphase in rapidly alternating clinging and negativistic behaviors. These alternating behaviors are the ingredients of what we designate as "ambitendency"—that is, as long as the contrasting tendencies are not yet fully internalized. This phenomenon may be in some cases a reflection of the fact that the child has split the object world more permanently than is optimal into "good" and "bad." By means of this splitting, the "good" object is defended against the derivatives of the aggressive drive. (pp. 107–108)

Mahler also points out that coercion and splitting of the object world, if excessive, are characteristic of the adult borderline transference situation. The rapprochement crisis with attendant splitting "may later become organized into neurotic symptoms of the narcissistic variety. In still other children, islands of developmental failures might lead to borderline symptomatology in latency and adolescence" (p. 229).

In the fourth subphase of separation-individuation, "on the way to object constancy," Mahler describes toddlers, especially in the third year, who show a tendency to split the object world, and for whom "mother in the flesh" (Bowlby 1958) or "the mother after separation" (Mahler 1971) is always disappointing. Self-esteem regulation is precarious. (Mahler, Pine, and Bergman 1975)

FURTHER CONTRIBUTIONS:
AN ANNOTATED LIST

The literature on splitting, as noted in chapter 1, goes back to nineteenth century psychiatry, but it is to Bleuler that credit is due for his pivotal monograph (1911). Jung, influenced by Bleuler, discusses splitting in "On the Psychogenesis of Schizophrenia" (1939). He is more famous, however, for his paired concepts such as anima and animus, female and male components of personality.

Freud's views on splitting have been examined by several authors; in particular, Stewart (1970) has reviewed the history of Freud's concept of the split in the ego and its relationship to denial and disavowal. Katan (1964) challenges Freud's view as stated in his paper on "Fetishism" (Freud 1927), and Pruyser (1975) has been more generally critical of the use of the term in contexts so varied as to stretch its meaning.

Pruyser (1975) is also critical of the psycholinguistic misuse of the term and explores its usage as a noun, adjective, and verb. Dorpat (1979) attacks the general use of the concept of splitting as a defense. In their 1973 review of the literature, Lichtenberg and Slap have found four categories for splitting.

Splitting in relation to borderline phenomena has been explored by authors other than Kernberg and Mahler, noted above. Green (1977) has related problems of discrimination in the borderline to splitting, and Horowitz (1976) has examined the cognitive and interpersonal-interactive aspects of splitting. Masterson and Rinsley (1975) have utilized Kernberg's conception of split ego and split object relations unit to correspond to a rewarding part-unit and a withdrawing part-unit. Bradlow (1973) has developed the thesis that ego splitting is key to the phenomenon of depersonalization.

5

The Experience of Splitting and the Splitting of Experience

It was Melanie Klein implicitly, and Fairbairn explicitly, who conceived of splitting as the manifestation of separate, dissociated personalities existing normally and abnormally within the self. While Freud's conception of the psychic apparatus (id, ego, superego) vaguely implied this, Fairbairn (1952) finally stated that all instinctual impulses represented individual egos and objects within the psyche. His notion, which eradicated the structural distinction between ego and id (holding that multiple ego complexes had their own "ids"), has found partial confirmation in the work of Lichtenberg and Slap (1973), who conceive of intersystemic suborganizations within the ego. These separate personalities within the psyche are organized around internal objects which have been created through splitting off, projective identification, and subsequent reintrojection. When these objects are internalized, they exist split off from other internal objects and from the self. They seem to have separate personalities, wills, and agendas, and they are therefore treated, particularly by Kleinian analysts, as though they are, in effect, separate people within the self. Kleinians do not understand the splitting off or projection of an impulse so much as a self or an object which personifies the instinctual drive.

CLINICAL EXAMPLES

Case 1

A forty-eight-year-old patient is a successful industrialist, married, and has three children. Important in his background is the fact that his mother became ill with tuberculosis when he was one year of age. He was separated from her for the next two years. She again became ill when he was seven years old and was again separated from him for about a year and a half. His general personality is warm, loving, gregarious, and outgoing. He is socially successful in the community and in elected public affairs. On the other hand, to those few who know him well, including myself, he is reticent, shy, and introverted. He has few close friends and, although wealthy, has an aversion to indulging himself in any way. Recently, he has been very depressed about his wife, whom he believes to have been unsuccessfully analyzed. He has complained that she is now more aloof than ever and wants nothing to do with people. He has also been critical of a nearby psychological sect which has been trying to convince children that parents and society are bad for them, and that they must avoid the influence of these noxious elements.

In one session, while complaining about his wife's withdrawal from people and about his son's belonging to this anti-society, anti-parent group, he also found himself complaining about an article he had read in the *New York Times* about Cary Grant, who apparently had undergone a "successful analysis" with LSD. Apparently, Grant had recovered the memory of feelings about his mother's abandoning him to enter a sanitarium when he was quite young. The patient became critical of Grant's criticism of women in the article, and also of his flagrant narcissism. His next association was a complaint about the small three-quarter bed he and his wife have in their bedroom. His wife had left her bed for his bed because of her bad back; his bed has a harder surface. The patient then associated to language and realized that words express thoughts but do not readily express emotions. He realized that his punctiliousness with semantics keeps him from having contact, not only with emotions, but also with his emotional selves, which *I* represent. He recalled this from a previous interpretation.

I was able to point out to him that his contumacious son, the narcissistic Cary Grant, and the anchoritic wife were ways of talking about different aspects of himself at the same time, that he existed in split selves as he existed in split thoughts and split emotions. His punctilious semanticism was indeed a way of keeping them separated yet allowing them to sleep together harmoniously albeit in a cramped space where there was no freedom for joy or self-expression. The patient confirmed the interpretation by realizing how much he was secretly like these other people but had a hard time accepting it.

Case 2

A twenty-two-year-old single female presented a dream in which I had come to her apartment in order to see her room-mate rather than her. She was very upset and depressed about this. Her associations to her roommate were that she was more dependent and needy.

I pointed out to the patient that the analysis was mobilizing her awareness of an aspect of herself with which she is not comfortable—a needy, dependent, infantile self which un-abashedly needs the parent. This needy self is experienced, I told her, as a split-off self disenfranchised from her own sense of being, but now she needs to reenfranchise it so that she can become more comfortable with her dependent vulnerability, rather than continue to affect a disposition of a pseudomature, overaccomplishing, hyperindependent person—all of which characteristics comprised the "false self" which brought her into treatment.

The experience of normal splitting and the normal splitting of experience may be seen as reciprocal phenomena which contribute to the mental homeostasis of the infant and also the adult. However, mental conflict is characteristic of the actual experience of splitting and being split. Repression and related mechanisms are unable to resolve the conflict through splitting off attention and consequent postponement of a solution. Instead, the experience of such a conflict constitutes an equivalent state of conative and affective war between at least two mental structures, each of which contains an "I"-"self"-internal object amalgam. Each "structure" behaves as if it were a separate human being along with colleagues, strangers, and opponents, all within the body of a single person. Conflict represents, in fact, the surfacing of a split which has already taken place. A patient entering analysis may be aware of some conflictual splits, but others surface as the transference regressively mobilizes them. In this instance, splits refer to states of incompatibility and asymmetry which are activated beyond a critical threshold of awareness.

Case 3

A forty-five-year-old systems engineer, logical and fastidious, has gradually become aware in his analysis that he thinks linearly and cognitively, but is relatively insensitive to feelings in himself and others, and he has become especially impressed by how little emotions figure in his thinking. A semantic and logical rigidity in his language effected a defensive redoubt which offered few apertures for feelings to get through from the inside or for interpretations to penetrate from the outside. It gradually became apparent, however, that his emotions portrayed themselves not in words but rather in visual images. When I offered an interpretation one day about his lifelong tendency to ward off his experience of dependency on mother figures, he negated it but then had a phantasy of a large and round, soft ball with an opening in it like a cave, into which a long, pointed knife was being thrust. Inside the cave were multiple ball-bearings. The knife apparently went easily through the spaces between the ball-bearings without harming them. It was quite some time before the patient was able to recognize that he had had a phantasy of a hostile projective identification into his mother's soft body to penetrate and kill the internal babies. This separation between the logical mind, which is represented verbally, and the emotional mind, which is expressed in visual form, also represents a severe splitting or isolation between two separate means of processing information.

Case 4

A thirty-seven-year-old general practitioner reported having experienced himself as being detached all his life. Being a father, husband, person, and physician were all unreal experiences for him. He nevertheless managed to acquire a family and the medical practice and continued a "Steppenwolf" existence until he decided, one day, to "break off" or "split away" from his previous existence. He quit his medical practice and divorced his whole family. In analysis, he finally saw that this "splitting off" from his family was an attempt to get out of the feelings of unrealness inherent in being a "split personality" in the first place. His schizoid existence, which was predicated upon splitting off his true feelings and living in the state of projective identificatory vagueness, a sort of unreal hibernation, so to speak, caused him to feel anesthetized to the world and, therefore, in something like a sensory deprived state. His splitting off from his family and from medical practice was acting out a need to penetrate the soft bubble of his vagueness and to enter life.

This patient began to realize one day that he circumscribed happy moments with his wife by separating them off from the rest of his life. He also began to realize that he was "playing games" with himself by keeping his professional life separated from his marital life, which in turn was split off from his hobby life. He began to realize that he was playing games in each life to keep them separate, and that each life was a private dream life vis-a-vis the other. Each life was two-dimensional. He was afraid to unite the splits to achieve the third dimension and realize the sadness and sorrow he had over the phantasied loss of his child self.

All abnormal personalities, as well as most so-called normal personalities, seek generally to exist as split-off selves in various

degrees of communicative integration or disruptive disharmony. Each split-off self behaves as though it has a separate
agenda or scenario which is as a rule unmodifiable—save,
hopefully, through analysis—by the agendas of other selves.
The "walls" between selves have developed because of *precocious closure* early in life, and thanks to a "hyperimmune"
response of the instigators, each enclosed self seems too over-
protected to be able to join the other personalities. Change
invites disapproval. In a patient who has been depressed all his
life, for instance, the "depressive self" is threatened by analytic
progress, and consequently may instigate a negative therapeutic
reaction.

Case 5

A forty-six-year-old physician was depressed, had been ha-
bituated to alcohol for many years, and was dilatory in his
relationships. Analysis had been successful with regard to many
symptoms and character traits but not with respect to his
dilatoriness or alcoholism. Finally, I came to realize that the
alcoholic split and the dilatory split were separate selves which
behaved along separate agendas. They would "permit" progress
as long as their own welfare was not interdicted. The motivation
of the alcoholic self, for instance, was simply to get a drink. "It"
did not care whether the patient was happy or unhappy. If the
patient was happy, "it" would inveigle him to get a drink in
order to celebrate; if he was sad, to console. "It" took advantage
of any state of mind to gain its own ends. The only way progress
could be made was for the patient to realize the very lack of
motivation in this personality—in the ordinary sense—except
for getting a drink. The realization of its extraterritoriality by
his more conscious sense of self helped pave the way for the
reduction of this trait as well as for the dilatoriness.

DEMONIACAL POSSESSION

Dissociation of selves is a phenomenon which, it seems to me,
is far more common than Kernberg (1975) has implied by

confining it to the borderline catgegory. It may go unnoticed because of the organization of the psyche which the *Background Object of Primary Identification* (the environmental mother or inherent self-object of autistic relatedness; see chapter 6) confers on the ego. But through a series of patients suffering from feelings of hopelessness, withdrawal, and intensive envy, a special category of dissociation of selves has come to my attention (Grotstein 1979d, 1979f). These patients, who also exhibited negative therapeutic reaction, all seemed to believe: "It is too late; there is no hope! I have already condemned myself." They behaved, that is, as though they were damned.

Common to all of them was the belief that they had, at one time or another in childhood and later, disavowed themselves in order to become invisible, so as not to confront some crucial experience. They believed that their self-forfeiture or disavowal had been achieved via a pact with the Devil. The principal effect of this pact was that they had given over their souls or bodies to the Devil in order to be safe and unnoticed but meanwhile lost ' contact with their selves. The phantasies about these selves were multifarious but seemed to cluster around the following possibilities: *(a)* the abandoned self becomes derelict and unclaimed and is then taken over by a host of nameless intruders. This phenomenon can be seen in hypochondria and other conditions. Winnicott (1952) and Laing (1960) have designated this the false self which is now disembodied by the true self. The phenomenology of this aspect is that this self is lost, derelict, worthless, condemned, and forever spoiled. *(b)* A disavowed self emerges which is projected into others and then experienced as always avoiding or turning its back in retaliation for having been rejected. *(c)* There develops a diabolical self which is the active, retaliatory aspect of the disavowed self which then seeks to reenter or recombine with the disavowing self in order to torment it and repossess it under its diabolical control.

The end result is the creation of separated personalities either within or outside the self (or both) which live in Hell alongside the disavowing self for the sin of betraying one's soul for the purpose of achieving omnipotence. The diabolical personality then begins to act as a "kidnapper" of the normal self and takes control. We can see this phenomenon especially clearly in psychotic illnesses where outrageous acting out seems to demonstrate the need for help which his ego cannot ask for directly. In my experience such calls for help are complex double messages instituted on one hand *(a)* by the trapped, kidnapped self which recognizes that it is disempowered and under the control of a separated, disabolical, mad self—and seeks to get help from the community beyond the self so as to get rescued from its mad jailer; and *(b)* by the need of the diabolically mad self (the jailer) to prove its triumph over the disavowing self, now its prisoner, and to assert its omnipotence flagrantly in the face of reason.

The psychoanalytic approach to these patients, as well as to those who demonstrate dissociative phenomena generally, must begin with the therapist's awareness that he is dealing with separate selves having different agendas, scenarios, and motivations.

AUTOSCOPY

The phenomenon of autoscopy is the illusion or hallucination of one's twin self-image. It is a specific example of a split in the self, and ordinarily reported to be quite rare. I have reviewed the literature in a separate contribution (Grotstein 1980a).

Autoscopy is characterized by experiencing one's double during hypnagogic and hypnopompic states. The image is translucent. Autoscopy may accompany a variety of states, including migraine, epilepsy, tumors of the brain (particularly in the parietotemporo-occipital area), in schizophrenia, and in normal self-contemplation. Schilder (1933, 1935) postulated that autoscopic phenomena represent a breakdown in the representation of the body image, whereas Todd and Dewhurst (1955) believe it to be a breakdown in the structure of narcissism. The experience of a twin self at sufficient distance so as to register upon the visual, auditory or kinesthetic senses is generally felt to be eerie and preternatural. It is one of the rare moments (though quite common in dreams) in which one can have that sense of experience of oneself at a distance where the separation and the connection combine to give an uncanny impression.

A typical example of the autoscopic phenomenon is as follows. A bright, highly confident attorney consulted me for depression, which quickly lifted in the analysis when I was able to interpret his fear of death as precipitated by his father's illness. As the analysis progressed, he informed me of how gifted and nonhuman an attorney he was, especially in court. He reported an incident in which he was cross-examining the adversary in court and was aware that he was a detached spectator observing his own brilliance. He would frequently observe himself and say, "Great job!" These episodes were frequent and seemed "almost visual" and sometimes actually were. Frequently, while he examined the witness or adversary, he experienced himself as an observer at the council table and also experienced himself as doing the examining. Interesting in this case, therefore, was the shift of perspective from the observer to the observed. He experienced himself as both the brilliant lawyer and the observer at the council table. While relating this to me, he stated, "My mind is now moving to the left, and I see myself lying on the couch and yet I can feel myself to be on the couch at the same time. I guess the maniac is watching the real me—or is the maniac the real me?"

This observation of self corresponds to his assuming the role of an idealized object admiring a grandiose self. All his object relations seemed to be superficial, expedient, and self-serving. He trusted no one but himself and developed the notion that he had had to be a parent to his own child-self, so to speak. This splitting was in the service of a manic defense against his true dependent feelings which his depression heralded.

We know from the work of Gazzaniga and LeDoux (1978) that the corpus callosum and the deep cerebral commissures do not myelinate until about four months of age and do not complete their myelination until adolescence. This means that the infant and child effectively has two brains and also maintains two consciousnesses, perhaps even into and throughout adulthood. It is my belief that autoscopy is a more common phenomenon than has previously been believed, occurs very frequently in dreams, and is due to a mysterious ability for the two minds to separate themselves sufficiently so as to achieve an eerie and uncanny distance. Freud (1919) discussed the same phenomenon in his paper, "The Uncanny."

CAPGRAS'S SYNDROME

Capgras's syndrome is the illusion of doubles and was first described by Capgras and Reboul-Lachaux (1923). Unlike autoscopic phenomena, in which case the self is perceived as its own double, the patient with Capgras's syndrome has the persistent belief that a person or persons have been replaced by doubles who impersonate them. It thus constitutes an encapsulated paranoid delusion, occurring, according to Lansky (1974), in an otherwise clear sensorium. Lansky goes on to state, "The clinical presentation is in sharp contrast to those in which misidentification is more generalized or appears as one feature of a global cognitive disruption" (p. 360). Like autoscopic phenomena, Capgras's syndrome is believed to be quite rare, but unlike autoscopic phenomena, it is far more pathological. Just as autoscopic phenomena involves depersonalization, Capgras's syndrome involves derealization, that is, an alteration of the percepts of the external world because of a more marked disruption in ego boundaries.

SOME EXAMPLES OF SPLITTING IN
PSYCHOSIS

The experience of being in splits is especially acute when split-off parts tend to reoccur as though they had traveled a boomerang trajectory and then press for reentry into awareness. The return of the repressed, which actually is the return of split-off selves and internal objects in projective identificatory reunion, may be due not only to repetition compulsion, but also to the basic cohesive primal oneness of primary identification. All split-off and projected parts of the self are fated to return to a primary oneness—thus, the hallucinations and delusions in psychotic experiences of persecution and *déjà vu.* The psychotic also seems to lack the instrumentality of rectification of imagery because of the damage to his capacity for secondary revision and elaboration (Grotstein 1977a,b). He consequently more keenly and concretely experiences himself to be actually split, and to be located in myriad places. This is the agony of psychotic fragmentation. The psychotic picture highlights what is less dramatically, but hardly less poignantly, experienced by most people at one time or another—the experience of being uncentered, loosely held together, and existing as many people in oneself. Being "beside oneself," "out of contact with oneself," and "sleepwalking" are all examples of this feeling.

Case 6*

A formerly hospitalized psychotic young woman had felt, throughout most of her life and during the early part of her analysis, to be in "bits and pieces." The following dream occurred in the termination phase of her analysis when she entered the threshold of the depressive position: "I was in Sunday School and was thirteen years of age and yet I also knew that I was really twenty-two, and therefore it was kind of like a dormitory or in a way it reminded me of a temple or a Sunday School class, as if it were 1963, rather than 1972. John Kennedy was still alive and I had a feeling of wanting to warn him that he was going to be assassinated. When I awakened from the dream, I experienced a strange smell. The smell seemed to be of Westwood Hospital [where the patient had been hospitalized at the beginning of her analysis]. I thought about how destructive I had been when I was there, and then I

---

*I am indebted to Dr. Duke Fisher for this case example from our supervisory sessions.

had a thought that perhaps in three or four years I might be able to have a child. I went back to sleep again and I had a dream that I was walking downhill. Then I woke up again."

Her associations to the dream were that over the weekend prior to the dream, her family had a brunch for her grandfather to celebrate his eightieth birthday. All the grandchildren and great-grandchildren were there. He gave a beautiful speech and she was proud to be a member of the family and felt that she really belonged to them—a feeling that she hadn't had for quite some time. She also recalled that she and her husband had taken her nephew out to dinner and she found that she was very fond of him, wanted to have a child of her own, and found that she was far less jealous of her sister, whose child it was, than she had been in the past. She then stated, "I never knew being with a child could be so good. He is very much like my father. I don't know why I never allowed myself to feel good about a child. There was a special movie on TV about battered children. I guess I feel like a child beater."

The therapist linked her being thirteen and also twenty-two, which was her age at the time of the dream. She was trying to bring her past life into alignment with her present life and to dissolve the splits so as to be continuous with herself: past, present, and future. She was also trying to undo and to repair her assassinating attacks against her father, as represented by John Kennedy in the dream, and to undo the violent deterioration and splintering fragmentation of her psychotic period at the beginning of the analysis, represented by the smell in Westwood Hospital. In addition, she wished to unite the battered child, which represented assassinating attacks against her own dependent self, with her present adult self which wanted to have a baby of her own. In short, she had existed in bits and pieces and had also felt split off on the outside from her family and other important objects, as well as split on the inside. The analysis was able to bring into alignment her needy, dependent self with the other portions of her personality on one hand, and also the relationship to external objects so as to achieve a sense of continuity and oneness. The splits had been united.

Case 7

A twenty-seven-year-old single psychotic male discussed splitting his relationship to women between two girlfriends, one a mature woman with whom he could have an adult sexual relationship, and also a young, naive, or ingenuous girl who would add another quality. He despaired of ever finding a woman who had both qualities, yet seems to require these two different types in order to have a complete love affair. One of the difficulties in having one or the other, he pointed out, is that it would give rise to a fear of the relationship being "lopsided." This then caused him to associate to two different kinds of friends. Back in his native town he recalled having rich friends which made him want to have poor friends and vice versa. This association continued in his relationship to food where he pointed out that he would like to have his food divided, rather than mixed together, because of his need for a sense of balance.

He also reported a fear of being unidimensional. When he was a manager of one of his father's factories back in his native town, he was too sympathetic with the people on the other side, and therefore was too balanced in order to be a boss, which required being unidimensional or off-balanced. He wondered whether his mania and depression were ways of balancing states of mind. He related this to his need for a background offset for foreground focus in concentrating attention when reading or in studying. In his phantasies he wishes to have two homes and two jobs in order to have opposites. When he was a writer he would write about opposite phenomena. He feels that he has a fear of things coming together.

Keeping things in equal and opposite splits ultimately became related, in subsequent hours, to having equal but separate relationships to mother and father. Eventually, he was able to experience himself as a "double agent" and realized that he always had tried to keep the parental couple split apart.

This same patient experienced another important splitting phenomenon—that of the mysterious twin—which persisted into adult life and occupied a great portion of his analysis. The mysterious twin occurred when he was about three years of age and seemed to have been conjured in order to ease his loneliness while playing. Later it became assigned omnipotent properties and would, for instance, always beat the patient in chess, checkers, and other games. Finally, he enfranchised it as the Advisor, a phenomenal and imaginative person who would go out into the world and make fortunes for the patient. In later life and during the course of analysis, the Advisor became the enemy of the analyst, as well as confused with the analyst at times. He would be the one who would give omnipotent interpretations as if they were oracular truths which had to be devoutly obeyed. It ultimately transpired that the Advisor was the patient's experience of his own ego-ideal combined with a mad, omnipotent self as described by Rosenfeld, and also an ideal object, as first described by Klein and Fairbairn. This formulation also corresponds to the later notions of Kohut and Kernberg. When the patient was able to experience the omnipotent nature of the Advisor and also to experience that the Advisor was himself, a most dramatic event took place in the analysis. The patient became visibly shaken, depressed, and nearly fainted. He then began to cry, with the realization that the Advisor was back inside himself and was not omnipotent. He felt deflated, little, hopeless, and together with himself for the first time. The splits had been united.

Case 8

Mindful of Bion's concept (1957a) of the difficulties schizoid and schizophrenic infants have in projecting their feelings into a defective container-mother, and mindful also of Meltzer's concept (1974) of the dismantling by the autistic child of his own perceptual apparatus so as to destroy the awareness of his needs in order to protect a mother felt by the child to be depressed, I interpreted to another schizophrenic patient that he felt unable to pour his feelings into me for fear they would overwhelm me and that I wouldn't be able to contain them. As a result he had to project them into a split-off image of himself—a "negative him." By "negative him" I meant a person who would remember to forget everything the patient did not want to remember. This seemed to be the most cogent interpretation I had given the patient in nearly three years of analysis. He then recalled that he had been afraid all his life to acknowledge to relatives that he did not recall certain well-known events in the family that could be called romantic. He believed that his mind had been altered. He felt very ashamed and mortified about the prospect of being caught and not being able to remember. He recalled several sad events which happened to relatives, events which had taken place within the seven-year period of the amnesia. He then had a visual phantasy about a rounded triangle which appeared to be flat and then achieved some depth with a tank tread as its third dimension with a ribbon wrapped around that periphery. He had an image of himself cuddling a wounded person lying on the bed, reaching out to him in order to help him or to offer him some kind of love and protection.

At this point I interpreted to him that he was now in contact with a belief that his needs had so damaged his mother and her breasts that he abolished the awareness of his needs by flattening them and also by flattening the image of the needed breast. He then banished them to his negative self so as to be permanently forgotten. Following this interpretation more memories began to emerge from the amnestic era.

It appeared that the patient was able to discover that, while a child playing around with thinking, as children oftentimes do, he could inconsequentialize experience by separating one brain from the other. My suggestive evidence for this second interpretation was that his associations in analysis were sometimes visual and were without verbal associations. The visual was cut off from the verbal, in other words. A flood of dramatic visual associations disembodied from their verbal translations seemed to be a way of talking about a storehouse or warehouse where his negative self had housed memories in visual form denuded of the significance of the experience.

6

Primal Splitting, the Background Object of Primary Identification, and Other Self-Objects

I believe that there is *primal splitting,* that is, the definitive experience of physical birth and the constantly repeating—in an effort to undo or deny—psychological birth.* Primal repression is the seraphim guarding the gates to the unborn state and helping to divide the self which experiences birth from the nonseparate continuation of primal identification. The experience of being in splits is mitigated by the experience of at-one-ment or self-cohesiveness which, in the language of experience, is achieved by actions emanating from the presence of the phantasy of what I call the *Background Object of Primary Identification.*

Clinical experience has convinced me that the Background Object of Primary Identification is a valid concept; it corresponds to a more primitive and inchoate version of the idealized parents as described by Freud (1908) in "Family Romances." I also believe that the Background Object is phantasied as the primal matrix from which we descend: it is the object behind us who rears and conducts us into adulthood. Sandler (1960) has referred to this concept as the "background of safety"; Winnicott (1965) termed it the "environmental mother" (as com-

*Parts of the discussions in this chapter require an understanding of projective identification, and the reader unfamiliar with that concept might first wish to read chapters 9–11.

pared with the objective mother); and Erikson (1959), as the "objects of tradition." Bion (1962b, 1963, 1965, 1967, 1970) has alluded to it as "inherent preconceptions." Kohut (1971, 1977) more recently has adopted the term "self-objects" to denote a state of partial fusion (symbiotic "siamese twin") relationship between the immature self and its caretaking object. It is my belief that the Background Object of Primary Identification is one of three self-objects. Later in this chapter I shall deal with the two other self-objects.

I postulate that splitting can be done (a) under the auspices of perceptual and cognitive thinking where discriminations are required; and (b) defensively, which involves momentary or permanent countercathexes against unwanted perceptions and feelings. Furthermore, I believe that the experience of splitting can be active as well as passive. Active splitting occurs as in (a) and (b), while passive splitting suggests the experience of helpless fragmentation beyond one's control. The latter form recalls the concepts of Charcot and Janet, who assumed a basic weakness in the personality organization of hysterics to be the cause of their split consciousness.

An object slowly and gradually discovered by the infant and child, the Background Object, can be conceived of as personification of the binding cement of personal identity. I am myself in the first instance because I know the ground I stand on and who reared me (sense of personal identity). The Background Object, consonant with the sense of personal identity, facilitates splitting in the service of thinking and perception, and (defensively) temporary postponement. On the other hand, a defective sense of a Background Object—probably precipitated by premature abruption of the sense of primary oneness—leads to a personality with a poor sense of personal identity and a sense of fragmentation and proneness to "falling apart." Moreover, precocious awareness of this premature abruption mobilizes a phantasy which denies being born, facilitating a pretense that their born self or separated self is merely an illusion, factotum, or "false self" (Winnicott 1952, Laing 1960), while the "true self" remains unborn. This unborn self exerts a powerful influence on its external representatives not to leave it behind; therefore, it seems to undermine any kind of developmental progression or success in life.

I first became aware of the Background Object in phantasies of patients with psychotic and narcissistic disorders, in which there was a common experience: that their backing seemed to disappear, or that they had nothing behind them, that they had no backbone, etc. One patient in particular related the instance of her three-year-old daughter having a nightmare while feverishly ill with flu. The daughter apparently awakened in the middle of the night seeing snakes everywhere, including the very floor on which she was walking. She ran to her mother's bedroom and mounted her mother with her back to the mother's abdomen. This was the only place where she could find relief. Although the mother, not the child, was the patient, her associations to the event soon established that she had identified with her child. She was the little girl who wished to lie down on top of me in order to get the "backing," protection, and "rearing" which she felt deprived of by her own parents.

After detailed inquiry into the phantasies and dreams of many of my patients—especially those who are in contact with the imagery of their "language of experience"—I have found two separate relationships to a Background Object of Primary Identification. One relationship involves sitting on the lap of the Background Object where the latter is behind it, and in the other the self is standing behind the Background Object with the implication of hiding behind its power for protection. The first corresponds to Kohut's conception of the grandiose self and the second corresponds to his notion of the idealized object protecting the infantile self.

Frequently I have heard dreams from analytic patients in which they were driving a car from the back seat. The associations to these dreams almost invariably led to a notion of having a defective backing and consequently, difficulty with autonomy. A borderline patient revealed to me that he had a recurring nightmare throughout much of his life in which he could see a plain surface in a dream and would then experience the surface "wrinkling into many split craters." This represented the deterioration of the smooth surface of his dream screen which I perceived as synonymous with the Background Object of Primary Identification.

From the analyses of several patients with narcissistic disorders and psychotic illnesses, I also became aware that the particular cogency of their narcissistic complaints was that of the absence of "perfect room service." Several of the patients were able either to dream or to phantasy that they wished to have a highly idealized object behind them on whose lap they could sit and whose power they could feel, but they would not have to be aware of the importance of this object face-to-face. In other words, they could take this object for granted. Taking the object for granted, and not looking at it, is implicit in the concept of identification. Whereas in object relations one is facing the object which is facing oneself, in identification, on the other hand, one is identified with the object in such a way as to see things the way the object does; in short, one is parallel and congruent with the object and is therefore looking in the same direction. Separation from the object disappears, but the purpose of identification, which is the acquisition of the power of the object and the invisibility of the vulnerable self, is achieved. The power of the object is then felt to be behind one, and it is and assumed, presumed, and taken for granted. The object *behind* can also be felt to be *underneath;* it therefore becomes the paradigm for the commonly used word *understanding.*

From another standpoint we must account for the nature of what Erikson (1959) calls epigenesis, the organizing template for future development. I believe that the conception of epigenesis of inchoate consciousness, and of an inchoate sense of space (inside-outside, up-down, etc.), requires a superordinating notion of a developing infant and an object from which he phantasies himself to be emerging. My conception (Grotstein 1979a,c) of a dual track—primary identification on one track and incipient separation on another—helps to account for a plausible notion of earliest infantile existence. The Background Object of Primary Identification is the guardian of inchoate

object constancy from the very beginning of life until representation of objects can replace the presentation of objects (self-
objects, internal objects), allowing for transformation of the
Background Object into a deitylike concept associated with a
superego and ego-ideal.

The infant's acceptance of separation from the object permits
a beneficent adhesive identification with the object, which
means—in terms of psychical spatial arrangements—that the
infant imagines himself to be sitting on the lap of this object or
juxtaposed in front of it. Acceptance of this separation with
subsequent identification seems to insure a sense of separate
and separating skin—that is, a skin-boundary container which
defines where there is a common amalgam of emerging self and
of the object from whom one has emerged. An acceptance of
this first boundary seems to vouchsafe secondary boundary
formations, which are the beginnings of categories, differentiations, and cognitive and perceptual splittings corresponding to
the principle of distinction. Subsequent normal splitting is a
function of the acceptance of this first splitting, while pathological splitting can be seen as a denial of it. (See Bick [1968] and
Meltzer [1975] for adhesive identification.)

ABNORMAL SPLITTING

The Background Object of Primary Identification underlies
the sense of security and one-ness in all individuals. With this
primeval object as its heritage, the personality can conduct
meaningful splitting operations, perceptual or defensive, in a
way that is clean and relevant to its adaptive and maturational
needs. The personality without this heritage is, I believe,
doomed never to be freed from a primal sense of fragmentation,
disunity, and discontinuity.

Clinical experience with borderline patients has convinced
me that the phenomenon of mental dissociation, assigned by
Rosenfeld and Kernberg, among others, to such cases, reflects a
noncohesive conception of the Background Object. As a result
of its defective installation, different "split-off" personalities

may surface alternately or simultaneously, revealing a lack of psychic organization and unity. This is even more true in psychotic cases. And while the appearance of the mental organization of normal and neurotic cases seems to be that of a defensive repression of instinctual drives (classical theory) or of internal objects (Klein and Fairbairn), I believe that such patients also contain split-off subselves but, thanks to the integrating operation of the Background Object of Primary Identification and its maturational successors, these subselves are so repressed and organized into the framework of the cohesive self that their "rumblings" appear as impulses to be repressed. Borderline and psychotic patients are not so fortunate. The experience of a defective Background Object of Primary Identification does not offer these unfortunate patients that cohesive blanket of protection. As a result, patients who evince the presence of dissociated personalities show in stark relief the basic nature of the organization of the personality when cohesion does not occur (a montage of selves).

One borderline patient had a nightmare in which he had arrived at a radio station in order to call for help because of being pursued by a robber. As he approached the microphone in one of the studios, a sinister, shadowy person ran up from out of nowhere and grabbed the microphone from him and began to speak. The patient frantically exclaimed, "Someone has grabbed my microphone and won't let me speak." The patient associated to his belief that he was trying to cooperate with me but was not giving me the true story about his feelings and did not know how to do so. The dream added the missing element— that another subpersonality "grabbed the microphone" whenever he really wished to get help.

When I speak of the Background Object of Primary Identification, I should make it clear that it begins to emerge when primary identification begins to dissolve gradually into separation-individuation, especially in the phase of rapprochement, although the process may take years if not a lifetime for a significant portion of the Background Object to be divested of primary identification. We encounter the Background Object in many phases of life. I felt the concept to be necessary, as I stated above, to account for the rudimentary coherence of the inchoate infant prior to attaining what has often been called *"object constancy,"* by which is meant the awareness of the constancy of an object in the child's internal world which corresponds to a real object in the external world. One of the most striking examples of the function of the Background Object, I believe, is its role in ego integration and the construction of dreams, and as author of the scenario of analytic hours.

We take for granted that the neurotic patient free associates in a determined manner in which coherence is implicit so that the analyst can rearrange the associations according to his metaphoric template, give interpretations, and expect them to be accepted by the patient's reasonable mind and to be rejected by the natural forces of resistance which generally yield in turn to interpretation. As we all know, we are not quite so fortunate in borderline cases and are particularly unfortunate in psychotic cases. It is my contention that the Background Object is responsible for the organization and coherence which allows free associations to have that kind of unity which lends itself to analytic integration. In psychosis the Background Object of Primary Identification is fragmented and scattered, and the absence of its function can be noted in the relative looseness of associations.

Metaphorically, it might be useful to understand the Background Object in terms of Hooke's Law. Hooke's Law of physics states that the stress on a solid substance is directly proportional to the strain produced, provided the stress is less than the elastic limits of the substance. The Background Object can be seen as the phantasy of a unifying container whose elasticity is tested by mental content. If the stress exceeds the capacity of the container (Background Object) to adjust elastically, then strain develops to the point of rupture, fragmentation, or implosion. Schizophrenics respond to stress by fragmentation; manic patients may rupture or explode; and depressives may implode when they become psychotic.

OTHER SELF-OBJECTS

The Background Object of Primary Identification is but one of three major categories of self-objects and can also be thought of as the Background *Subject* of Primary Identification since it is experienced as part of subjective "I"-ness—our subjective sense of security and confidence. The second self-object was discovered by Tausk (1919) when he pointed out that the newborn ego chooses its own body self as its first object. This self-object concept owes much to Freud's (1914b) conception that the id chooses the ego as its first object. Thus the *self* is experienced by subjective "I" as its first object and is therefore entitled to "self-object" statehood.

Kohut's self-object is an interpersonal or external object into which newborn "I" projectively identifies itself in order to establish a feeling of symbiotic protective unity. It is therefore secondary to the Background Object of Primary Identification and is achieved only through projective identification. One of the major tasks of this secondary self-object is to orchestrate the relationship between the other self-objects on track one of continuing primary narcissism with the separate "I" on track two (of the dual-track, which I will explicate shortly). Experience has taught me that children and patients seem to think of the womb mother as different from the mother whom they "know" through their senses. Many patients have experienced disruptions in their early childhood, for instance, in which they were moved from home to home but were always with their parents. Nevertheless, the loss of the environmental womb mother was experienced as traumatic despite the fact that they were in contact with the object mother (interpersonal self-object).

I refer to Kohut's self-object as being formed by projective identification. This is true for both aspects of the bipolar self-object conception. The mirror object seems at first glance to be a separate object which merely reflects the self's grandiosity, but, on another level, it is believed to be the possession of the grandiose self and is felt to be there solely for its purpose. Here we can use the symbiotic paradigm of the siamese twin (two separate heads and a continuous body) in order to account for this dual concept. The self's idealized relationship to an idealizing object more closely corresponds to a merger transference, which I call the "papoose" relationship insofar as, pictorially, it can be represented as an infant basking in the glory of its idealized object and is partially fused with that object as well as partially separate. The merger relationships and the twin relationships are similar. The merger relationship implies more nearly total projective identification into a state of at-one-ment with the object, whereas the twin relationship reflects a splitting off of an idealized aspect of the grandiose self (or other aspects of the self) and their projection into a corresponding prototype in the interpersonal environment.

Another case example of a defective Background Object who also demonstrates two separate aspects of projective identification is one I have used in this volume in another context (chapter 5, case 6): briefly, a middle-aged physician who was alcoholic, dilatory, withholding, and passive-aggressive. When he was five years old, the father took the whole family (mother and children) for an itinerant tour of the plains states which extended over three years. This was done in the service of the father's professional work as a historian. Although the patient was with his family throughout this time, his personality seemed to have undergone a depressive withdrawal, after which he became reticent, introspective, apathetic, and dilatory. In the analysis several dreams emerged which revealed a poor background support of safety. He was perennially on the verge of fragmentation.

SELF-OBJECTS AND INTERNAL OBJECTS

I now wish to return to the discussion of self-objects to point out their relationship to internal objects. Klein's and Fairbairn's conceptions of internal objects correspond to Kohut's ideas of self-objects. Despite the fact that the implications of each seem to be so different, I believe that they constitute different aspects of the same phenomenon. The term self-object, as the hyphen hints, suggests a state of fusion (actually, partial fusion) of the self and the protective interpersonal object, in Kohut's usage. This self-object is a combined object concept and constitutes a representation of and by subjective "I." ("I" experiences its self in a state of partial fusion with an interpersonal object; if there would be total fusion, there would be no experience since there would be no "I" separate enough to experience the fusion.) One of the more important implications of the self-object conception is that self is *not* an individual but rather is symbiotically *binary,* like siamese twins.

Internal objects, on the other hand, are thought to be structures *within* the self's ego. They are formed by projective identification of aspects of the self onto and into interpersonal objects with subsequent introjection and secondary (internal) identifications with them. Classical analysts prior to Kohut had no notational system for archaic objects and therefore called them *archaic object images* (Jacobson 1964). One's experiences of self-objects *or* internal objects give one feelings of safety, security, confidence, and self-affirmation on one hand and danger, diffidence, and self-consciousness on the other. They are inventories of self-assessment.

The conception of "internal" object requires more rigorous reexamination, however. Interpersonal objects (external objects) are not taken into the psyche via introjection until the self projectively identifies aspects of itself into or onto them first. The interpersonal objects must be recognized as being identical or similar to preconceptions of them before they can be realized as objects. By virtue of the fact that the primitive self can relate to interpersonal objects *only* through projective identification (through the assignment of similarities of self to object), then there is always a state of fusion or partial fusion between the self and the interpersonal object, at least initially. By virtue of the self being in a state of projective identification with its object, to the extent that a state of fusion exists (on one track), then the object cannot be taken in because there is no ego boundary separating the self from its object to confirm "in" as distinguished from "out." Yet there may be a feeling of "taking in" on the separate track, the track two of the siamese-twin symbiotic model.

I hope the reader is able to follow this seemingly labyrinthine exercise in logic. Its importance is far-reaching. If what I am saying is correct, then the self-object is a clearer way of denoting that the individual who is employing projective identification in the creation of internal objects exists in a binary state of symbiotic partial fusion with an object rather than in a state of separation as an individual. The ultimate importance of this concept is that the symbiotic state (not to mention the autistic state) is an important state of relationship which normally persists on one level of mind long after the individual has achieved separation-individuation status in the depressive position of rapprochement. Thus, finally, an internal object is identical to a self-object and can be thought of as being located within the psyche on one track and to be a continuing experience with an interpersonal object in a state of partial symbiotic fusion on the other.

THE DUAL-TRACK THEOREM

I have gradually become convinced from my clinical experience and from rethinking psychoanalytic theory that it has become necessary to invoke a new way of regarding mental phenomena. (Grotstein 1980e). The work of Gazzaniga and LeDoux (1978) has shown that we normally have two consciousnesses, each a referent to a cerebral hemisphere, and the consciousness of one hemisphere superordinates the consciousness of the other in order to give the impression of a single consciousness—much as with the two eyes, the two ears, etc. In psychotic, borderline, and other dissociative states, the "binocularization" may break down into a "diplopia," so to speak, in which case the component selves are all the more apparent, especially without a Background Object of Primary Identification to cohere them.

I believe that the dual track applies in many other ways as

well. Klein's concept of initial infant mental separateness collides with Mahler's (and others') conception of continuing postnatal primary narcissism or primary identification. The dual-track theory allows for each to be correct on two tracks—one of separateness, and one of continuing primary narcissism or primary identification. We can now think of normal autism and symbiosis as continuing permanent stages which exist side-by-side with states of separation-individuation throughout life. The infant may go back and forth between the two tracks as playful mastery or states of danger motivate it.

The importance of this for splitting phenomena is obvious but is more subtle for projective identification. When the infant experiences projective identification with an object, the character of that object is twofold: *(a)* the object is transformed by virtue of that aspect of the infant which has been split-off, disidentified from the self, and reidentified in the object. For instance, if envy is the quality which has been split-off, and reidentified in the object, the image of the external object has been transformed into an envious or denigrating object which is then internalized and installed within the ego; and *(b)* the second transformation of the image of this external object is the result of the more direct *impact* of projective identification on the object. For instance, if the infant was envious, then the envious attack can result in a damaged or mutliated object, the latter of which is also introjected and identified with in the ego. This gradient in the ego comprises two distinctly separate levels of object formation, ego objects, and superego objects, constituting Freud's bipolar melancholic paradigm (Freud 1917b).

The dual track helps us to understand two separate states of self-awareness which are disconnected and therefore split-off rather than harmonizing in the normal dual-track conception: *(a)* the ego identified with mutilated objects comprising the depressive core of the self; and *(b)* the superego comprising aggressive identifications which influence and attack the ego and its objects.

Throughout his career Freud seemed to have a love-hate relationship to his discovery, the unconscious, particularly in regard to the id and the instincts. The dual track allows us to conceive of the pleasure principle and the reality principle as harmoniously complementary rather than merely at odds with each other. They are two separate and equal ways of processing the data of experience. The dual track also helps us reconcile the existential polarities of being unique *and* ordinary (in the sense of being human) at the same time. Psychopathologically, it is difficult to keep both in balance.

7

Attacks Against Linking: The Phenomenon of Blocking of Thoughts

There is sufficient evidence to suggest that the infant's mode of thinking is animistic, magical, solipsistic, and personified. "Thoughts" are people or phantoms prancing about an inner stage. The thought known as "hunger" can be the phenomenon of being stalked by a malevolent predator from within—the greedy breast, for example. Thoughts originate, in other words, as personification of experience via projective identification or, if I may modify Alfred North Whitehead, thoughts create themselves, as personified objects. "Thinking" consists of arranging objects as pawns of circumstance on some imaginary chessboard in the mind. This is what Freud meant, I believe, when he said that thinking was experimental action. Originally, this action is external physical action and is kinesthetically organized in a manner termed by Piaget (1952) "the concrete operational stage of sensorimotor development." As the concrete sensorimotor (kinesthetic) operations become "metabolized," they carry with them a kinesthetic shadow of the sensation of external objects. Facts getting together would then be indistinguishable from objects getting together.

When Klein (1945) extended the oedipus complex to the oral phase of the first year of life as a mythic paradigm of "thirdness," to use a term of Peirce's, she was, in other words, structuring the circumstances of the first world of the infant by using the oedipal myth to account for a feeding couple in harmony, and the third object, a stranger, who intrudes upon or sabotages this harmony. This saboteur originally may be greed, envy, or hostility; it is quickly assigned by the infant to the intruding stranger—father or sibling. With thirdness, a middle space has been created in which the infant can experience the nurturing object, threats to that object, and the relationship between it and the object.

In pathological splitting, the infant, by virtue of precocious access to the instrumentality of the ballistic force of the death instinct,* attacks the objects which frustrate him directly and also attacks the links or associations between himself and the object. According to Bion (1959a), an attack against the perception of the breast (and later the penis) is an attack against linking organ of communication. This psychic murder of linkages is akin to denial or disavowal and is a primitive massive splitting which alienates awareness of connections between infant and object. By extension, all linkages become objects of attack as well. This is the prototype—according to Klein (1952a), Rosenfeld (1952), and Bion (1959a)—of an attack against parental intercourse, known as primal scene anxiety. In other words, any of the mother's possible sensuous linkages with other objects is perceived to be a danger, and therefore is subjected to envious attack. Since thoughts are objects and objects are thoughts, this attack against linkages of people is akin to attacks against the mental representatives of them and their internal linkages. Thus, if the thoughts cannot get together, then the parents cannot get together, and vice versa.

Bion (1959a) has emphasized that the breast and the penis are

---

*In another publication (Grotstein 1977a,b), I have redefined the death instinct as the inherent undifferentiated defense organization. I conceive of it as an organization like the libidinal and epistemophylic organizations, as an inherent structure which contains the programming of the prey and the predator. In other words, it contains the capacity to recognize fear and deal appropriately with danger or extinction. Aggression and destructiveness are the instrumentalities of this defense organization. Normally, it is quite harmonious and cooperative with the libidinal and the epistemophylic instinctual organizations.

not merely part objects, but are actually *linking objects,* that is, linking organs to whole objects. They therefore symbolically represent the relationship's between self and object and between objects—and also the *significance* of these relationships. Therefore, primitive attacks on the representation of the breast or penis constitute the vehicle whereby links between objects are severed—and this results in attacks on the capacity to link thoughts and perceptions. Furthermore, different components of the perceptual, cognitive, and affective systems may be severed. Bion points out, for instance, that a patient may have so deployed his visual system that it functions like a mouth, a hand, and an ear, thus disenfranchising the operations of the other sense organs and precluding "common sense," that is, the capacity for the senses to communicate freely.

This attack on links amounts to rendering experience inconsequential; the significance of facts for truth undergoes eclipse or extinction. It is tantamount to destroying the architecture of the three-dimensional world and experiencing a flattened world of two dimensions where significance is muted (Grotstein 1978). Bion (1959a) suggests this happens in an infant who is to become psychotic and also happens in the mental world of adult psychotics.

Peto (1977) has made an important addition to our knowledge of attacks on linkages by suggesting that the disharmony between positive and negative hallucinations allows the latter to run rampant. Negative hallucination imaginatively negates the linkages between self and objects and between object and object. The consequence of this silent negation is the creation of objects which, stripped of their capacity to relate, can only agglomerate through pathological condensation. Peto's conception reminds one of Conrad Aiken's poignant story, "Secret Snow, Silent Snow," in which the poor victim descends slowly and inexorably into a softened, silent, snowy but destroyed internal world. The apocalyptic "calm" of the psychotic's world seems to be the result of this silent but deadly negation, of autonomous negative hallucination.

CLINICAL EXAMPLE

A twenty-seven-year-old general practitioner, a single man, complained that he could not talk to people or originate conversation, and had difficulty in thinking about most things. Many years of analysis brought out that he had experienced feelings of strangeness all his life, suffered from a "learning disability" during latency, and generally seemed to shun people. His style of free association was unusual; it resembled the circumspect and labyrinthine course of a sinister and elliptical oracle. My questions, interpretations, and confrontations would seldom be attended to directly; he would get to them, if at all, paragraphs later. His overflow of associations also showed this pattern insofar as he would get to a point, get away from it for quite some time, then tentatively return to it and develop it a little further. He gave pronouncements rather than associations, thus the oracular quality. Ultimately, analysis revealed that he believed himself to have suffered an "infantile holocaust" in which his capacity to think and to speak was impaired. Thus, his generation of thought and of speech was curtailed. He had to wait for longer periods of time to be able to recall the lost link or to forge new ones. This gave a clumsy, formal, high-mannered quality to his speech which was even poetic at times. He could not organize his thoughts, so he pronounced them as independent statements of position. This patient ultimately experienced being cut off or "unlinked" with himself. He spoke of himself once as though in a *Star Trek* episode, condemned to be alone in outer space forever, stuck with his anti-self to whom he could neither defeat nor submit.

During an hour with this patient in which subtle attacks on linking became evident, he arrived fifteen minutes late. He stated, "I have not too much to talk about today. Not much has happened. I could talk about being late. There is something not kosher about being late. It gives me a chucking feeling as if I have done something wrong. I suppose that's due to old habits or religious customs. Rituals are important, and coming on time is one of them. But from the purely utilitarian standpoint, it doesn't really matter. So what am I left with? Seemingly meaningless rituals which permeate me. I could have been here earlier; I could have gotten up earlier. I really decided to go to get an estimate on the damage to my car and I was pressed for time—but what does it matter? I gambled and I don't know whether I won or lost. I had to compress thirty minutes into fifteen. I wonder if I left the light on, on the stove.

"Maybe my dream kept me up. Don't know how to talk about it. There was an oration in which four of five people were participating. I recognized my uncle and myself. The first part was good; the second part was boring. There was a bizarre scene in the next dream in which there was a hugh trellislike structure made of redwood. The trellis was supposed to be God. I climbed it and then, while I was climbing, I had thoughts about primitive relationships and relative development of children. At first there was one God, and then there were two Gods; then there was God and his mate. While I was climbing the trellis, I was fighting with God; this time I was thinking of cosmogyny. In the next moment, I was also having intercourse with God, which was an alternative cosmogyny. The one God was an earlier development. The trellis was an unstable structure, and I was climbing quite high and I thought I might fall off if I wasn't careful.

"Five of us had to give various talks on different subjects. I was anxious about mine and wasn't prepared. I care about getting my car fixed—no, I'm worried about the wedding. Maybe getting a marriage license today bothered me. I worry about things being crowded—and also of being comfortable. The tables in the dream were either too few, and it would be uncomfortable, or it would be too many and it would be crowded. *I must give you words without images—on the other hand, I have images without words. You keep the words and I'll keep the images. Perhaps my landscapes are private—no trespassing!* Perhaps there is also a large guard dog at the gate. Toothless perhaps . . . "

Although I had inferred that his relationship to his girlfriend was deepening and that marriage was discussed, this was the first I had heard that the marriage license was an accomplished fact. I knew about his car accident so I could understand the reference to its being fixed. He intermixed the latent and the manifest content of both dreams in a desultory and confused manner. His account of merit in the battle with God and the subsequent sex with Him was without any reflection on how unusual it was, even by dream standards. His statement about imagery without words and words without imagery gets to the heart of the matter, however. "Images without words" are the archipelagos of visualized associations long since denuded of words and contexts—a lost continent of consensual meanings, long since overwhelmed by the chaotic tides of primitive catastrophe. The eyes are no longer talking to the ears. It is now quite impossible for him to let his eyes express feelings and thoughts to his auditory organization which is responsible for the transformation of images into words so as to communicate to me, the analyst, who must hear with my ears and relay to my other senses, mainly sight and touch. I, in turn, must retraverse this difficult road with words which are alien to his eyes. His eyes and ears cannot make common sense together. My eyes and ears, which make sense to me, can only be attacked by the forlorn envy of eyes which cannot hear and ears which cannot see. The result is splitting of the linkages of thought.

I do not wish to convey that I believe this patient to be *resistant* to analysis, as that term is conventionally used. On the contrary, I mean to convey the poignant agony of a seemingly "blind" and "deaf-mute" patient who is trying with utmost difficulty to relocate a consensual alphabet lost a long time ago in a holocaust, and who now exists in an annihilated state in which he despairs of analytic help, yet does not give up.

This patient also demonstrates attacks on linking in terms of the therapeutic alliance. Although he "associates" in the hour, his "associations" have no meaning, he claims, nor do my interpretations. There seems to be a glass wall separating us. Moreover, my own attempt to formulate interpretations in my own mind is experienced as being attacked, so that our external relationship (link) is attacked, and my internal relationship to him is attacked. In terms of the representational world, this internal attack can be visualized as his attack on his conception of the relationship of my self-representation (analyst representation) to the patient representation in me. He has had multiple dreams in which the severance of this internal relationship within me has been damaged. Moreover, I can confirm this from my own projective counteridentifications.

Another attack on linking in this patient is seen from a much more subtle vertex. Bion (1950) has discussed the differentiation between the psychotic and the nonpsychotic parts of the personality in schizophrenics, and elaborated a special instance of this in his paper on "The Imaginary Twin." In the cases of schizophrenia which I have analyzed, I have frequently encountered the phenomenon of the mysterious twin which represented either an omnipotently perfect aspect of the personality or the psychotic self. In most cases, however, there seemed to be some connection between the two—that is, they were on speaking terms. Kernberg has discussed this as split representations which he believes are pathognomonic for the borderline state. The patient I have been discussing, however, shows considerable evidence of multiple personalities but there seems to be no connection between them. The violence of his hatred for, and antipathy towards, the analysis and the analyst, and disavowal of any progress over many years, belongs to one personality which seems cutoff from another personality which, when not in my presence, has fond feelings about the analysis. It took me many years to be able to learn about the feelings of this second personality.

INVARIANT INTERNAL OBJECTS

Attacks on linking, therefore, are attacks on the communicating organs, the sense organs of the infant individually and collectively, and the linking organs of the parent, basically the breast and the penis, which metaphorically become parental thought and concern. Attacks on linking affect the infant's sense organs individually and collectively, and also his perception of his parents' thinking internally and externally. The internalization, then, of a *thinking couple* (to use Bion's term), which includes a projecting infant and a collecting parent, is therefore attacked and severed so that neither perception nor thinking really takes place. There are only the agglomerations of pseudothoughts. The phantasies involved in this phenomenon are associated with the formation of invariant internal objects.

I have discussed invariant internal objects elsewhere (Grotstein 1977a, b); with respect to attacks on linking, there are four: (1) the obstructive object; (2) the defective boundary object; (3) the magus object; and (4) the exciting or stimulating object.

The *obstructive object* will not contain projections and will attack thinking and linking whenever they appear in either the patient or the object to whom he is trying to relate. The obstructive object can also be thought of as a defunct *scavenger object,* one who cleans up the infant's (or object's) mess.

The *defective boundary object* results from attacks on the objects of thought. The patient may feel himself to be poorly defended or, quite typically, haunted with shame and afraid of blushing. (Incidentally, in my experience the fear of blushing is quite characteristic of psychotic and borderline patients and has to do with a phantasy about their skin container being defective; identification with a defective boundary object leaves them feeling porous and open to the malevolently voyeuristic stares of others.)

The third internal object resulting from attacks on linking, the *magus object,* is experienced as oracular, dooming, sphinx-like. It is hovering, sinsister, and threatening, and its role seems to be to remind the patient that he cannot think or link, and to confirm this fatal flaw whenever it appears. This phenomenon is so typical of psychotic experience that I have termed it the magus object in deference to John Fowles' novel, *The Magus,* in which a Zoroastrian sorcerer who is pictured on one of the cards of the Greater Arcana tarot symbolizes the qualities of the mysterious Dr. Conchis. Dr. Conchis ("conscious"?) was an analyst who superimposed his own life themes on his patient for the latter to work out. I believe that the magus object is formed by a projective identification of the epistemophilic instinct into an object in order to get rid of the entire mental apparatus responsible for curiosity, growth, and investigation in a way corresponding to Bion's description of the formation of bizarre objects. In other words, not just thoughts and feelings but the mind itself is believed to be projected by the psychotic. Because it is believed to have been split off, the container for the split-off mind now reprojects the alienated, eerie themes onto the patient for him to live out. This is really the return of his own life theme and epistemophilic instinct in disguise. The sphinxlike nature of this object is a testimony to the original attacks on the patient's capacity to speak and to be spoken to by other objects in active, normal communication. Thus, the magus object becomes sphinxlike and relates to the schizophrenic in eerie "hints."

The fourth internal object which forms as a result of attacks on linking is an *exciting object* or a pathologically *stimulating object*. This phenomenon is much like the reconstruction of a mannequin, as in the movie, *The Stepford Wives*. This object, apparently idealized, perfect, and yet in effect dead, nevertheless seems to be a source of powerful lifelike radiations of vitality and enthusiasm for these patients, particularly the patient discussed above. It is akin to the worship of idols in religion and to drugs or other manic talismans in more nearly normal cases.

Blocking or attacks on linking, then, are attacks on the very inchoation of thinking by the infant and the psychotic, initially because of a stimulus barrier which is defective or diminished due to inherent or constitutional forces or to an insufficiently protective maternal-paternal-family environment. Curiosity about the self and about outside objects is experienced, according to Bion (1957a), as emanations from the self into the object via projective identification. When the projections from the self and the object intercepting the projections are both reintrojected, the infant has a model for a "thinking couple"—a "pitcher" and a "catcher," so to speak. The "catcher" not only "catches" but also sorts out the "catch," thinks about it, categorizes or generalizes upon it, and resorts utlimately to mental action. The feedback to the infant about the object's handling of the "catch" is decisive for the establishment of sanity. Too low an inherent stimulus barrier may cause the infant, for instance, to project inordinately, to the point where he actually seems to project his capacity to register sensations and code them into feelings—the *primary process* (Freud) or *alpha function* (Bion). The infant is robbed not only of the apparatus with which to engender thoughts and feelings, but has created an altered, damaged, and bizarre object out of the part object, the breast— the prime linking organ of infancy. The result of this projection is the formation of a breast which now contains: *(a)* the violently attacking and splitting aspects of the infant's mental apparatus (the death instinct, or, as I prefer to call it, the inherent undifferentiated defense organization in its inchoate form); *(b)* the greedy, possessive, and insatiable aspects of his libidinal needs; *(c)* the results of the damaging attacks, (e.g., a mutilated breast). If in addition there is poor boundary formation due to defective adhesive identification, the result would be the formation of a *bizarre object* which has elastic boundaries and seems to swell with the enclosed expanding contents. This bizarre object, in turn, seems to haunt the infant or patient, attacks his linkages, or sucks them even further. It then becomes internalized in the recovery phase as the nidus for smoldering schizophrenic "infection." It constitutes one of the prime characteristics of schizophrenia, known as *bizarreness.* The schizophrenic tries to circumvent this phenomenon by yielding to the object's attacks on one hand and secretively splitting it off in order to cooperate with the therapist on the other.

The schizophrenic exists in splits. These may be split personality organizations, but can also be splits within the split organizations. The picture I portrayed above concerning bizarre objects would be an example of a splitting within a split-off psychotic "organization." The relationship between the psychotic self and its clustering delusional objects represents a split between self and object (as well as object and object) due to fragmentation. Yet, at the same time, the self maintains some awareness of contact with these objects. The same is true of the maintenance of the awareness of contact between objects themselves. Tausk (1919) clearly demonstrated this eerie phenomenon of bizarre splitting coeval with bizarre connections in his elaboration of the "influencing machine" (see chapter 10). In discussing its formation, Tausk pointed out that patients suffering from this delusion invariably seem to believe that the machine is controlled by sinister forces or objects who are the estranged (split-off and projected) aspects of benign, friendly objects. The latter suffer the fate of the patient because they are more clearly identified with him. This picture constitutes a paradigm of the structure of psychotic narcissism. Narcissism, as I have pointed out elsewhere (Grotstein 1977a,b), is an object-relations state in which there is a relationship between an "I" and an object with whom the self is partially confused (self-object presentation). The objects comprising the "I," which is already separate and *re*presentational, are themselves *re*presentations, that is, "spirits" of the released objects. The self-object presentations constitute unreleased objects.

A hospitalized schizophrenic woman told me she could not remember the image of her analyst, who had had to interrupt treatment because of his own hospitalization for surgery. I had known that the patient related to her analyst, who was in supervision with me, in a most tenaciously parasitic way. She did not wish to make progress for fear of losing him. She could not tolerate separation from him and therefore could not establish her own separateness. Consequently, she could not preserve the space reserved for him in his absence so that the "hallucination" or conjury of his image could take place. Her two relationships to him, therefore, were as an idealized and possessed object, on one hand, and an absent, unconjurable object on the other, in place of which was a bad object which constituted an evil image of him made up of her greedy and envious projections and then reintrojected as an evil Dr. M———, who became ill in order to punish her.

Normal narcissism is itself a split relationship between "I" and a self-object presentation, the latter which constitutes the confused and undifferentiated aspects of self and object. In abnormal states, narcissism may be more clearly split between "I" and self-object because the integrity of "I" begins to disappear, and a defensive polarization then occurs.

It is important to point out again that each split appears to be a semi-independent personality organization and therefore has its own good-bad, idealized-contentious criteria. Because of alternating or shifting perspective (Bion), the newly formed "I" can identify with what we would call the good split and condemn the bad one, or can identify with what we would call the bad one but which the "I" can psychotically call the good split. In short, the bad split does not know that it is bad because it has the other split to condemn. Kernberg (1975) has ignored this obvious point in his delineation of the split in the borderline personality. Rosenfeld (1978) and Bion (1970), on the other hand, have made significant note of it.

Concurrent with the formation of this new walled-off split another process seems to take place—*generalization*. Generalization, the opposite of splitting (differentiation), follows the splitting in order to "repopulate" the newly formed cosmos in a harmonious manner. A case example is as follows: A twenty-eight -year-old psychotic patient ran away from his home town in an eastern city because of an enormous persecutory anxiety. The city had become all bad, then "always had been all bad," and the people in it all bad. There were no redeeming features. The people, in particular, were greedy, selfish, and envious. The girls were all "Jewish-American princesses," the women were all spoiled "bitches," and the men were conniving and evil.

It finally dawned on the patient, following my interpretation about the splitting-off and projection of his Pittsburgh self into Pittsburgh as a safe warehouse for his disavowed feelings, that he was treating all the people there as if they were separate but undifferentiated ants in a homogenous ant colony. He realized he had generalized them so that they would not have the individuality which would require him to continue to make distinctions and to think. Since all Pittsburghers were "evil Jews," all he had to do was to avoid that city and he would be out of harm's way. This concept of precocious closure and generalization seems operant in all obsessions, delusions, and phobias. It may very well be operant in all symptoms.

REVERSIBLE PERSPECTIVE

Bion (1963) has cast new light on attacks against linkages from yet another, more obscure angle by invoking the paradigm of perceptual illusion known as *reversible perspective*. This refers to a perceptual phenomenon in which the background can become foreground and vice versa. The most commonly used example is that of a silhouette of a vase which can alternatively be seen as two profiles. Bion employs this term to designate a split or rupture in communication between patient and analyst (as well as between two or more people generally) in which the premise inherent in the discussion between the two is not agreed upon although neither participant may know it. The analyst may be offering an interpretation which suggests the premise of the faces, whereas the patient may have assumed his associations to have had the premise of the vase. The patient may agree with the logic of the interpretation on one level but not accept it on another, a fact which may be opaque to the analyst and even to the patient.

Reversible perspective suggests a split in perspective within the patient and a split or rupture in perspective premise between analyst and patient—and maybe even between patient and patient. Most commonly this occurs, in my experience, in patients who seem to have a false self which offers a tenuous and tentative relationship to the outer world while their main focus of mental activity is within an autistic self. A psychotic patient offered me multiple dreams nearly every day for years but would be disturbed by my interpretations and by my attempts to give interpretations even though he often saw their logic. It gradually began to dawn on me that this was a patient who was dwelling in "the domain of -K" (Bion's term for the altered internal world created by transformations in hallucinosis). His "dreams" and "associations" were dysymbolic "beta elements"—mental contents suited for evacuation via projective identification but not suited for storage, deciphering, or thinking. His premise and mine were at variance. The genesis of this tendency toward reversible perspective was a primitive infantile mental catastrophe, I believe, in which he thought himself to have so attacked and mutilated his image of his mother's breasts that he could no longer link thoughts or feelings, experience the significance of events, or relate to people. In short, he had become virtually autistic.

In general, one can find this in many analytic hours, particularly with psychotic and borderline patients, where the analyst may feel disoriented because the patient is shifting the focus of associations. When the analyst gets a tentative conviction about a "selected fact" which the patient seems to be talking about, and then offers an interpretation, the patient then seems to treat the interpretation indifferently, almost as if it were a fly landing on his forehead which he brushes away insouciantly while pursuing another track of associations, leaving the analyst bewildered or disoriented.

Langs (1978) has recently written on this same subject in reference to disturbances in the bipersonal field. He provides the interesting analogy of color blindness where the analyst can see the numbers set in "camouflage" within the controversial color scheme background whereas the patient cannot. The premises for each would therefore be different. Reversible perspective seems to be a special form of attacks on linking which is characterized by an attack on "shared focus."

PREMATURE CLOSURE IN NEUROTIC CONDITIONS

Premature closure is also familiar to us in everyday clinical practice in what Bion (1965) calls the *constant conjunction*. Any accompaniment to a trauma, according to Freud, seems to be able to be included in a fixed way with the trauma. Constant conjunction is a more nearly accurate way of stating the problem of traumatic fixation. It predicates a constant union in the mind between two elements or more which ordinarily would have been independent of one another. A girl who has experienced rape in her youth may associate all men to the trauma of injury, forming a constant conjunction, and, therefore, a premature closure of two elements which, but for circumstance, might have been forever unjoined. Premature closure in this instance is the insistence of a harmful bond between two elements and, at the same time, upon confrontation with one of the elements, conjury of the other. A great portion of analytic work thus evolves into painstaking *resplitting* of constant conjunctions which have been split off into the unconscious.

Thus, premature or precocious closure is what I term that aspect of splitting which intrudes into differentiation too early, closing off the differentiated aspects in such a way as to preclude any further influence upon them (Grotstein 1977a,b). In particular, it is my impression that the schizophrenic suffers from the differentiation between his abnormal personality and his normal one; the former is closed off so early that it has not participated in the maturation of the normal personality. This "closing off" is much like an encystation of a pulmonary tubercle which lives in the state of extraterritoriality to the normal self. In milder cases, prejudices or rigid preconceptions which do not change with new evidence would be examples. Obsessions and phobias would be typical clinical examples.

ATTACKS ON LINKING IN NEUROSES

Attacks on linking can also be seen in hysteria, phobic states, and obsessive-compulsive neuroses. Obsessive-compulsive patients in particular attack linking by displacing the focus of attention away from the real to a false point and do their best to sever any connection between the two. The incessant doing and undoing for which this disorder is famous has to do with the intrusion into awareness of the distorted thoughts which have now become omnipotent and the incessant countermanding attempts to ward them off. All efforts of the obsessive-compulsive patient are to attack the links between self and that which he wishes never to see or to know. In proportion as these objects of perception are continuously denied and split off, they in turn attack the patient when he tries to think about other things. As a consequence, the obsessive-compulsive is reduced to the compulsion to doubt.

The phobic patient attacks linking by attempting to perpetuate a distinction between a safe and an unsafe object which, after the distinction is made, becomes generalized and then contained. The good or safe object is experienced generally as having a definite outer defense perimeter beyond which lies the dangerous or bad object. Because of claustrophobic anxiety attendent upon continuing a relationship to the safe object, however, the hapless patient is constrained to visit the dangerous object in order to renew the safety of the safe object and diminish claustrophobia in relationship to it.

The hysterical patient attacks linking through the polarization of goodness and badness so that, according to Fairbairn, the idealized object is outside, the bad object is inside, and the patient identified with the latter. Intercourse, whether sexual or mental, does not exist transactionally as a reciprocal mutual feedback between two people. The idealized object is a magus which is oracular and functions through pronouncements. The patient seeks to find an ideal solution and identify with it. Conflicts are "resolved" by being split off or dissociated into another personality or into the body as a conversion. At any rate at least two separate noncommunicative entities seem to be relating to each other in a nonmutual manner. The variations correspond to Bion's basic assumption groups (see chapter 11) within a work group insofar as one object overcomes the other object combatively, sexually, or parasitically.

The principle of distinction then can be thought of as governing the differentiation of the container and the content (the infant's inherent givens and the data it is to work upon) and their respected descendents. At the same time the container and the content undergo generalizations upon each distinction. This principle of mental organization can also be thought of as the principle of dialectical perception and dialectical cognition, analogous to Hegel's dialectical idealism in which there is a thesis to which is opposed its antithesis, and the distinctions are resolved in a reconciling synthesis. Stierlin (1969) has gone in great detail to apply Hegelian dialectical reasoning to infantile development.

8

Mental Dissociation

Dissociations in the personality often reflect alternating, mutually contradictory states of mind, especially in the borderline. Oftentimes they are experienced as people who are possessed or kidnapped, much as in demoniacal possession (Grotstein 1979d,f). The following case may well demonstrate this. A thirty-five-year-old woman who was born in central Europe and whose childhood occurred during World War II had been suspicious of intimate relationships ever since she was very young. She divorced her husband after accusing him of mentally tormenting her. Then she married another man who was in the same profession only to leave him after about six months and return to a quasi-liason with her first husband. In the second courtship with him she insisted on living apart and would relate to him alternately as loving, seductive, and warm and as cruel, castigating, and rejecting. Her husband apparently put up with this cruel attitude for a long time because he remembered that when they were first married she had been a beautiful and loving wife. He told her that he believed the good her had been kidnapped and was under the control of her more evil personality which acted like a devil or as if possessed by the Devil. He also told her that he believed the good personality he saw in her now was like a "decoy" in order to lure him into continuing a relationship with her diabolical self. The transference seemingly reflected the correctness of her husband's allegations; indeed, I could detect alternating, contradictory states of mind in which she would appear as altogether different persons.

The molar splits or dissociations of mind in borderline and narcissistic patients often may not demonstrate this alternating, mutually contradictory nature, however. Patients with profound disturbances of self-cohesion may actually experience themselves as split selves, but the contradictory nature of these variegated selves is blurred or eclipsed by compromised reality testing which ignores distinctions. We can readily observe this ego-syntonic personality blending of split selves in eccentric patients who, for example, talk to themselves as they leave an analytic hour but seem otherwise to behave as if they were perfectly normal. They may hallucinate or experience delusions of influence and still be able to carry on as if they were integral persons. This ego-syntonic form of dissociation is obviously subtle and probably due to an adaptation out of futility to a compromised and constricted level of mental functioning.

The more obvious dissociation is characterized by mutual incompatibility or contradictoriness of the splits. One patient in particular demonstrated this: A thirty-five-year-old single female who was a nurse by profession, after experiencing severe migrane headaches which did not yield to medications given to her by her family doctor, was urged to consult a psychiatrist whom she disliked intensely because he wanted to take her into analytic psychotherapy rather than simply treat her for her headaches. She was referred to another psychiatrist who offered to treat her psychoanalytically but had no time and consequently referred her to another therapist. When she saw the third therapist she broke down completely and, owing to the fact that the third therapist was not a physician, was re referred to the first doctor, whose office was at the hospital where she became a patient. When the three therapists got together to discuss the case, they were amazed at what different stories they had obtained. One had got a normal history of a person who had neurotic conflicts with her mother and father, another therapist got the story of delusions of influence whereby she was under the power of a religious family, and the third therapist derived a history of a poor relationship to peers and to the opposite sex. One piece of evidence from a friend of hers came to the attention of the managing psychiatrist after hospitalization. The friend said that the patient had seemed to be perfectly normal until she began complaining that the computer she was working with "spoke two languages." Subsequently, in her hospital course, she was able to confide to her physician that she was terribly scared of a split-off aspect of her which was "evil and mad" and wished to influence her to kill herself. She explained she was in great danger when she tried to cooperate with the doctor. This is a typical example of gross dissociative splitting which one so commonly finds in borderline and psychotic patients in analysis.

DISSOCIATED PERSONALITIES

The case of absolute dissociation is better known to most people as "multiple personalities," in which there appear to be completely separate personalities, one having no knowledge of the other. But the analyses of narcissistic, borderline, and even neurotic cases have caused me to increasingly regard the phenomenon of splitting from the vantage point of dissociation and to suggest that the phenomenon of dissociation of personalities is more widespread and universal than has hitherto been thought. Freud himself must have known this, as Fairbairn so cogently reminded us, when he talked of an ego, an id, and superego as separated and dissociated components of the psychic apparatus.

Case One
A thirty-four-year-old single woman who had just completed graduate professional training was unable to start her professional career because of an inability to pass the qualifying examination and also because of a great fear of inadequacy. She appeared to be a will o' the wisp who had innocuously wafted her way through life without ever really occupying it. Early in

the analysis it gradually became obvious that her innocuous, underwhelming, "false self" hid another personality which she knew about but could not produce on her own; it could only be produced frustration caused by another person or by circumstances. The patient was afraid of this personality because of the trouble it could get her into, but it seemed to be an effective one in terms of getting her through interviews for jobs, though it would not remain long enough to allow her to consolidate her employment. As a consequence, her passive self would predominate.

Important in her infantile and child development was the obtrusion of an older brother (she actually had two older brothers but only the elder of these was the "culprit") who apparently had a "minimal brain disorder" and who hyperactively dominated and controlled the household. He also threatened with his fists, broke his mother's arm, and once tried to stab his father with a knife. It is quite possible that my patient's primary oneness with mother was quickly ruptured and that mother herself was so worn out from taking care of the "problem child" that she had little to give her daughter. The patient herself seemed to have grown up in a trancelike state, attending a private boarding school in another country and then a distant state university, as if she were going through a routine without involvement. Crisis was precipitated when she graduated from college and did not know what to do or where to do it. She wanted to get married, but, despite her inordinate beauty, she did not know how—that is, she did not know how to meet men or, once she met them, how to hold onto them. She would be very exciting with men on rare occasions, and they would become fascinated, but after becoming involved in the relationship, she would become extremely helpless and passive and would seemingly disengage. The splits in her personality were organized around dissociated lines in which separate personality entities would portray themselves at different times. More important for my thesis here, however, is that she demonstrated that particular dissociated phenomenon which I have called the persistence of the unborn self. The first two years of her analysis were replete with memories of the abject terror of her brother and her resentment toward her parents for not sending him away to boarding school. As best as the patient and I could reconstruct her past, it appeared that she reacted to her brother's terrifying intrusions by running away into a private inner world of "calm"—the word she used most often in analysis. She began a lifelong pursuit of "calm" which supported her aimless drifting through a European girls' high school, a midwestern university, casual relationships with men, and a failure to make an occupational commitment. When finally faced with the issue of being an adult and unmarried, she reluctantly opted for law school only to regret it after she graduated. She then became aware that she wanted nothing more than to be married and have a family, and felt she had been cheated of this opportunity.

Even though she always remained loyal to the analysis and made sacrifices for it, she seemed not to have made much progress during the first two years. I became aware that she had conceived of me as a protective Background Object for her to lean up against for that kind of adhesive identification which Bick (1968) and Meltzer (1975) discuss. My interpretations were listened to, "mouthed," and forgotten. She always had a hard time remembering what we had talked about in any previous hour. I gradually became able to decipher this narcissistic transference after several dreams. In one dream she was pursued from the rear on the freeway by a mad driver. She quickly got off the freeway (with him in pursuit) so that her companion, another woman her same age, could escape. In another dream she and a boyfriend were sitting in a car, upon which a mysterious intruder attacked her and then pointed an accusatory finger towards her boyfriend. In the third dream, she was trying to get to her apartment when she realized that it had been taken over by some other girl—and she, the patient, felt despondent, lost, and dispossessed.

These dreams, the associations to them, and previous material from earlier analytic hours finally offered me the opportunity of suggesting to her that she was haunted by an alien voice which was also herself on another level of being. I told her that this alien self was her "unborn self," the one she gave life to every time she ran away from reality and sought "calm." The patient seemed to respond to the notion that her running away or turning her back on painful feelings and on the objects associated with them did in fact have the consequence of giving birth to phantasmal objects which imagination had transformed into voices or images of great power. She then reported that she was haunted by voices (inside, not outside) which seemed to have a strong influence on her. I then interpreted that her unborn self had seemed to become a separate entity with a separate agenda, consciousness, and motivation—the latter of which was to maintain the "fiction" (or reality) of its unborn state.

The purpose of the already separated personality was to be a vassal or a factotum to the unborn self to preserve its security. If the separated self was in great need or agony, then its pitiful cries would easily betray the unborn self and its longing for perfection, symmetry, and calm. Therefore, the separated self was under injunction to rid itself of its needy, vulnerable, and caring characteristics via denial (projective identification and splitting). On the other hand, success and progression were also inimical since they were incompatible with the nonprogressive, unborn, static self. Progress only enlarges the gulf between the two aspects, leading to many varieties of implosive catastrophies, such as the success neuroses, the negative therapeutic reaction, acrophobia, and countless other conditions. The patient's separated self had the unenviable task of negotiating Scylla and Charybdis in order to avoid two dialectical disasters and thereby to please two masters: the fictional truth of the unborn self and reality.

The day following these interpretative interventions, the patient reported to me that she had left my office after the last analytic session, crossed Wilshire Boulevard against exceedingly heavy traffic, and was almost hit by many cars which had to skid to a stop in order to avoid her. The patient seemed immensely impressed that she had a self inside which was out to murder her and that I had indeed been correct in my interpretations. The motive of the murder was her listening to my interpretations and deciding to let me help her in a new way. At the same time, the motive for a dangerous activity could be seen as an action in support of the hypotheses my interpretations had offered. My pointing out the very existence of the unborn self activated it as an internal saboteur of the patient's progress. It later turned out that this "unborn self" was a seemingly dead aspect of her personality that remained dormant when the patient made no progress but was excited into activity only with progress because of its fear of being left behind in the patient's forward momentum. Upon her reunion with it in subsequent stages of the analysis, she felt more whole and was able to make more meaning out of her internal and external life. The whole course of this analysis was fundamentally changed by this illumination.

I wish to emphasize that this patient's "active" and "passive" personalities were quite distinct, independent, and well-formed despite the fact that they were somehow intercommunicative. The agendas and scenarios of each were quite different. Her active self was so confused by an identification with her troublesome brother that she could not integrate it with her passive self. The two personalities remained at polar contrast until quite recently. The passive self, on the other hand, contained two distinct subsplits. One of these was a passive-dependent-symbiotic self which claimed to enjoy visiting her mother in Florida where she would be waited on and taken care of completely. The other one was a self which experienced extreme claustrophobia, hated being engulfed and smothered by mother or by boyfriends, and wanted to be "left alone."

Case Two

I have already referred to this patient in another connection as the psychotic patient who had developed the conception of a twin self in early childhood which later evolved into a delusional "Advisor." This patient had developed so delusional a Weltanschauung from so early an age that apparently, as best as I can reconstruct, he had become precociously oedipal in his relationship to his parents. (This is a finding characteristic of those who later become psychotic.) He developed the notion that his poor pathetic father was contemptible for having to arise early each morning and leave his wife in bed while he went out to make a humble living (the father was a successful industrialist)—leaving her to the patient who, as a child, would crawl into bed with her as soon as Father had left.

Beyond the apparent "oedipality" of this idea, the patient saw the opportunity of crawling back into bed with Mother as a way to use a pseudogenital mode to obtain possession of her. This secured for him the feeling of absolute security that he had, via his intrusive sexual phantasies, entered her so as to remain unborn. The ultimate simplicity of the meaning of all his subsequent sexual activities with girlfriends devolved, apparently, to this leitmotif. His "Advisor" was a variation on the same theme. The Advisor began as an imaginary companion and acted as his factotum in the external world while he remained alone in bed with mother. It would conduct his affairs in the outside world so that he could maintain his cherished illusion that he was "unborn." By the time he had consulted me for psychoanalysis, he had already left home. and become involved with several "fly-by-night" schemes to make money, and finally was ruining himself in the commodity market. His single goal was to make enough money to buy the richest house and the most beautiful of women to fill it so that he could preserve the illusion of paradise.

It became clear as the analysis progressed that his "psychotic" father had been viewed by him through the highly prejudiced lenses of his "evidence collector" self, an agent of the unborn self. By this time the Advisor had become the unborn self and had set up "shop" in his inner self and had changed from the obsequious earthly factotum into the cunning, diabolical dispenser of bad advice which borrowed of mania, easy solutions, quick changes of position, and desecrating ventures in the real world; in short, it became his undoing.

Eventually I was able to catch hold of the "evidence collector" aspect of the Advisor and was able to demonstrate, in the transference and in the historical material, that the patient was able to use certain actions and activities of his father to justify his position that his father had hated him and did not want him to be born. This reinforced preconception facilitated the eclipse of countless kindnesses his father had been responsible for. The patient's realization that he had distorted a lifetime of perception of his external objects in order to underwrite a psychotic insurance policy to be indemnified as being unborn (and therefore exempt from death and frustration) produced a salutary depressive deflation of his omnipotence which provided the necessary groundwork for meaningful analytic work.

Case Three

I should now like to offer some detailed notes of an analytic hour with a patient in analysis who suffered from mild neurosis and was never, in my opinion, psychotic or borderline diagnostically. He nevertheless demonstrated a mental dissociation in the analysis in which his free associations seemed to come from separate personalities with separate scenarios. His associations demonstrated a hypnagogic, trancelike state which allowed for the emergence of split-off selves. I became fascinated by this phenomenon early in the analysis when, upon first beginning to demonstrate this dual origin of associations, he said: "Now I'm leaving this story and I'm climbing through the television screen into another story." The following is as accurate a recording of the hour as I could make, and my interpretations, I trust, are self-explanatory.

PATIENT: What's going on now? I woke up exhausted this morning. I had a good full night's sleep. I had six hours sleep and that's usually quite sufficient for me, although I went to sleep extremely disturbed because L——— couldn't lie down without coughing—really coughing badly. I have somehow got to get her to stop smoking. And finally, she realized she was keeping me awake and she went into the other bedroom. But, all day I've been in a state like exhaustion but I have no reason to be exhausted. And then on the way over here I almost fell asleep in the car on several occasions. Once I almost drove off the road. So, I don't know what that means or if it means anything. Immediately [yawning] I connected that to the million-dollar offer yesterday. Then I connected that to success, and I thought I was upset this morning because I hadn't heard from B———— and A———— on the project. And we had a meeting at 11:00, and I figured I was just really exhausted because I was extremely anxious. Well, they came in and they both just loved it to pieces, and they really think it is going to be a success. They feel terrific and love my ideas for the project I want to sell. It's just all . . . it just couldn't possibly be better than it is at the moment. What's terrible? You didn't say anything did you?

THERAPIST: No. Did you think I did?

PATIENT: I heard you say, "That's terrible, that's terrible." As I said "What's terrible," I realized you didn't say anything and that it was in my head.

THERAPIST: Yes. So you assigned it to me. In other words, if things go well then where is terrible? Hiding behind good.

PATIENT: When I heard the "That's terrible, that's terrible" I was on my way to do or say something important. I forgot what it was but I knew what it was when I started the sentence.

THERAPIST: You see, I think that I am believed to find it terrible when things for you are good. I'm felt to be very jealous and envious of things being good for you if I'm left out.

PATIENT: If you're left out I feel you to be envious and therefore dangerous.

THERAPIST: Right.

PATIENT: [Pause] Oh, I went through a whole fantasy some-how about what a good guy my father is—how he wouldn't do what the other people in my fantasy were doing. He'd really do it right whatever it was I was dealing with, I can't recall. I realized that that was all bullshit because all I really wanted was to buy this clothing change at the store where L———— , M———— , and I were—

THERAPIST: Clothing change?

PATIENT: Is that what I said?

THERAPIST: Yes.

PATIENT: Oh, I think the clerk spoke rudely to me. And I really needed, really needed some clothes. So . . . we're walking away from her. We're on a beach. Something important like a statuette that has power of some kind—left it on this little hill.

THERAPIST: A statuette?

PATIENT: Yes, I think. And now I have to explore some Christian religion to find out about it.

THERAPIST: Well I believe the statuette is felt to be something like a spiritual icon, and perhaps some way of holding onto some symbol—well, of my spirit during the vacation.

PATIENT: How do you mean that?

THERAPIST: Well, I mean I'll be gone for a week, and I think you may be wondering how to find and hold onto some statuette or icon of myself. One time when you were a child maybe it was a blanket or a doll or some plaything. And it somehow or other contained the spirit of mommy when she wasn't there—or father.

PATIENT: I seem to be really centered on this mining community, this mountain impoverished mining town and this cave-in in the mine and everybody knows down there L——— and I are high and safe on a Saturday night. So, a waitress came to our table with a perfectly cooked order exactly the way I wanted it. I related that to this absurd frustration I have. We were going to make poached eggs in a pan. Have you ever done that before? I'll be damned if I can . . . if I'm making omelettes I can just take eggs in one hand and whack them on the sink and open them and never break the yoke. I must break four for every one I open for poached eggs. It's very hard today. I really just keep drifting away.

THERAPIST: I wonder if you're drifting away from the awareness of my drifting away from you?—on my vacation. In other words, it is as if you've already taken a vacation from my vacation by going into a state something like hibernation into the mines underneath the ground, but there's a fear even then that it may cave in. And you become aware once again of feeling the depression.

PATIENT: Why am I feeling the depression?

THERAPIST: My leaving.

PATIENT: And that's caused me to be in this tailspin all day, you think?

THERAPIST: Yes.

PATIENT: I'm scared. Huh! I'm supposed to go see these kids improvise tonight. All I want to do is go home and curl up in bed. Boy, it seems like such a waste of our last session but I know it's all grist for the mill. Is it possible for one flavor of metaphysical flavor of a number to seep into another fifth story of Manhattan Center?

THERAPIST: I'm sorry, I didn't understand.

PATIENT: What did I say?

THERAPIST: That's what I'm asking. I don't know. I didn't quite hear it. Something about Manhattan Center.

PATIENT: About what?

THERAPIST: Manhattan Center.

PATIENT: I wonder what that is. It might be . . . I might have meant Lincoln Center. I was thinking about theaters and I was thinking of N——— and my usual thoughts of not liking it.

Throughout the rest of the transcript of this and of other hours the patient wandered in and out of a hypnogogic state. The material conveys the impression that he is in contact with at least two and oftentimes more distinctly separate personalities which are in loose connection with one another. The dynamic significance of this dissociative phenomenon has to do with the pertinent crises in his immediate life which it is difficult for him to confront directly.

Interestingly, the patient reported to me that his mother and his younger brother were also hypnogogic from time to time. Thus his own dissociativeness may have been an identification with each, particularly his mother. Clinically, I believe this phenomenon to be a manifestation of a defective self-structure which, instead of containing him, caused him momentarily to fragment. Possible neurological contributions have been ruled out.

Part Two

Projective Identification

"Intuition is the sympathy by means of which
we project ourselves into an object in order
to achieve identification with that element in
which it is unique and which is
inexpressable"
Henri Bergson, *An Introduction to
Metaphysics,* 1913.

9

The Nature of Projective Identification

Projective identification is a mental mechanism whereby the self experiences the unconscious phantasy of translocating itself, or aspects of itself, into an object for exploratory or defensive purposes. If projective identification is defensive, the self may believe that through translocation it can rid itself of unwanted, split-off aspects; but it may also have the phantasy that it can enter the object so as to (actively) control it, or disappear into it (passively) in order to evade feelings of helplessness. As such, it follows the principle of generalization, corresponding to Freud's condensation, which accounts for the unification of objects on the basis of their similarities, contrived or natural. It thus is the counterpart to the principle of distinction which governs splitting.

In its more positive sense, projective identification is responsible for vicarious introspection and, in its most sublimated form, for empathy. It can be seen to operate in such processes as anthropomorphization and personification; it is active in romantic experience; and from it issues the impact of warnings, advice, and persuasion. As a primitive mechanism of communication it exists first between preverbal infants and their mothers, but is also residual in adult life as a form of affective communication. It is of prime importance to authors, educators, ministers, artists, as well as psychoanalysts.

Projective identification is implicated in states of confusion, disorientation, autistic detachment, claustrophobia and agoraphobia, and phantasies of controlling or being controlled by objects. Object relations under the influence of projective identification are characterized by coercion, manipulation, ensorcelment, seduction, intimidation, ridicule by imitative caricature, and martyrdom. Patients who feel that they are "sleepwalking," "possessed," or acting like "zombies" and "robots," are afflicted with projective identification. Telepathy is another example.

It is important to realize that projective identification is an unconscious phantasy, in effect, *imagination*. Employed defensively, projective identification rids the contents of one's mind or, when the experience is severe, the mind itself. An object, hitherto separate, becomes either the container for the alienated and negated contents, or confused with it through identification. The self utilizing projective identification may:

(i) return to a dedifferentiated state of fusional oneness with the nurturing object (autistic projective identification), blurring the distinction between self and object and between inside and outside;

(ii) invade an object in order to control it or be controlled by it, thereby eliminating feelings of helplessness (symbiotic projective identification);

(iii) evacuate or disavow aspects of itself into an object or objects in order to further the aims of splitting;

(iv) externalize aspects of itself so as to recognize analogous objects as familiar and identify with them (inchoate perception and thinking);

(v) scan the environment for objects which link up with aspects of itself (exploration);

(vi) communicate to other intrapsychic aspects of itself as well as to external objects (interpersonal projective identification in the service of object relationships).

Thus projective identification can be thought of in two distinctly separate categories: *(a)* externalization, which is projective identification into or onto an object without transformation of the self or the object; and *(b)* defensive projective identification which invariably results in a transformation of self and of the object. Externalization results in growth, maturation, and self-transcendence. Psychoanalysis is a specific instance in which free associations can be thought of as projective identificatory externalizations which allow the patient to grow through externalizing his inner mental content for interpretation, leading to self-assessment. Projective identification in the service of defense causes a transformation of the self and of the object in which the self may experience confusion, disorientation, denudation, emptiness, devitalization, and vulnerability to ideas of influence and control by the object (being in a trance).

It must be remembered that, for projective identification to occur, there must be a conception of a container into which the projection can be sent. In other words, there must be an object which has depth so as to be able to contain the projection (Meltzer et al. 1975). Bion (1959a, 1962b, 1963, 1965, 1970) conceived of the idea of inherent preconceptions (e.g., a breast) which can be thought of as not only filling one with nurture, but also as containing one's evacuations. Klein's conception of the "toilet breast" (1940) corresponds to this entity. Later in this contribution I shall deal with the isomorphism of projection and of projective identification. In the meanwhile, I should like to make a few comments about the nature of the container in projective identificatory experiences. Although I believe that projection and projective identification are identical, as I hope to establish later, I do believe that it is a very different experience if the infant believes it has projected unwanted mental content into an object and believes that the object has benevolently and effectively transformed the projection rather than having been subjected to transformation *by* the projection. If the object has transformed the projection and has remained unchanged, then the infant (or patient) feels a greater sense of safety and confidence in the relationship. Nevertheless, it can be said that what was once identified within the self has now been translocated and reidentified within the object, but that the object has handled the identification in an effective manner.

On the other hand, if the object has been transformed via the identification, either in the infant's (or patient's) mind or in actual interpersonal reality, then the identificatory aspects of projective identification are much more glaringly concrete (real). The key difference would be that the transfer of identification from the self to the object is transient and fleeting in one case and relatively permanent and transforming in the other. Perhaps the key point here is that the infant or patient must experience the object as having experienced the projection (and therefore as *identified* with it) but hopes that the identification does not so transform the object into one's victim that one has created a persecutor.

PROJECTIVE IDENTIFICATION AND THE FORMATION OF INTERNAL OBJECTS

The internal objects which comprise the scaffolding of the archaic personality are formed via projective identification of aspects of the infantile self into the images of external (interpersonal) objects, which are then introjected into the developing ego. This occurs in a variety of ways. For instance, if a greedily hungry infant projects his greedy feelings into an object, the object is perceived as having been transformed into *(a)* a greedily devoured, used up object, and *(b)* a greedily devouring object. Both are introjected, but the victimized object is identified within the ego, and the devouring object becomes the superego, according to Freud's (1917b) melancholic paradigm. Identification with the victimized breast leads to feelings of depression, inadequacy, narcissistic mortification, etc. Identification with the greedy object leads to the installation of a superego object which is now believed to be devouring, insatiably demanding, etc. Feelings of envy would be similar and would lead to the introjection of an enviously denigrat*ed* object and to an enviously denigrat*ing* object. Insofar as objects are created which are amalgamations of their external qualities combined with the projective identifications of the infant, the internalized objects become complex. For instance, the infant may project greedy feelings into his or her image of the mother's body and therefore transform her into a greedy, demanding object who, in phantasy, swallows daddy's penis and thereby is transformed into a *combined object* whose clinical debut is as a *phallic woman*. The possibilities of object combinations are many. I have already detailed some of the invariant internal objects in chapter 7. I shall illustrate them in case examples in chapter 12.

As the infant develops, it reprojects these introjected projective identifications onto its perceptions of progressively more real interpersonal objects whose task it is to discredit them and thus diminish their importance, omnipotent credibility, and influence.

THE PHENOMENOLOGY OF PROJECTIVE IDENTIFICATION

Infants and patients who utilize defensive projective identification may experience states of confusion and disorientation. The confusion is experienced in terms of that aspect of the self which has entered into merger with the object, whereas disorientation would be the experience of that aspect which is denuded of the mind which has been projected and which is left behind. Confusion and disorientation are distinctly separate experiences but may appear simultaneously or alternately in the clinical situation.

One masochistic patient, for example, would frequently berate himself for minor "offenses" and would also be extraordinarily dilatory in his professional and social appointments. He lost track of time so much that he would be sometimes over an hour late for some appointments. He claimed that he disappeared into "lateral time" rather than being able to progress into forward time. His dilatoriness and experiences of lateral time correspond to his disorientation, whereas self-berating corresponds to his confusion with his wife whom he experienced as being severely antipathetic towards him.

Claustrophobia is one of the prime examples of projective identificatory confusion with an object. In the state of intimacy, one may experience such a great feeling of neediness for one's object that it is experienced, via projective identification, as being the split-off container of one's neediness. Therefore, one may then experience being so needed by that object that one cannot possibly escape. The experience is a concrete one of being located inside the body of the other and unable to escape. Alongside this feeling of being trapped within the other, there is also a feeling of spoilment of the value of the other because of its being identified with one's own neediness. *Agoraphobia,* on the other hand, would be the experience of that aspect of the personality which has fled from claustrophobic intimacy, leaving its projected self behind inside the object. The denuded self feels terrified of open spaces and feels that there is no boundary to hold himself in and must consequently flee back to the object. *Acrophobia* follows a similar pattern. Phobias in general, like paranoia, are specific phenomenological examples of trans-location of disturbed aspects of self-experience which, when translocated into external objects, are felt to persecute one from a distance.

DEVELOPMENT OF THE CONCEPT

Freud's interest in projection dates from his correspondence with Fleiss, and he recognized its importance for understanding paranoia as early as 1895. When, along with introjection, projection was formalized as a primitive mechanism in the "language of the oral instinct," in "Instincts and Their Vicissi-tudes" (Freud 1915a), the concept of projective identification was implied, although not named. "On Narcissism" (Freud 1914b), which had introduced the "ego-ideal," had hinted at a similar mechanism, and the discussion of identification in relation to narcissistic object relations in "Mourning and Melancholia" (1917b) laid further groundwork. Freud's keen insight facilitated understanding of the magical aspects of projective identification: when the ego treats itself in a way that implies it is identified with the object, then that treatment represents an action upon the object with which it has identified. Perhaps the best example of this occurs in catatonic schizophrenia, where, when a patient lifts his arm, he believes that the world with which his arm is identified will stop.

Although Victor Tausk refers to "identification through projection" (1919), the first use of projective identification as such occurs in the work of Melanie Klein, and the major impetus for the promulgation of the concept came through two of her papers, "Notes on Some Schizoid Mechanisms" (1946) and "On Identification" (1955). These papers reestimated Freud's view of earliest object relationships put forth in the metapsychological papers and recapitulated Klein's own theoretical contributions. She had recognized the major importance for identification of certain projective mechanisms which are complementary to the introjective ones and notes that the processes underlying identification were implied in psychoanalytic theory even before they were formally recognized. Projection underlies everday feelings of empathy as well as grandiose fantasies (e.g., Christ fantasies)—both of which are familiar kinds of "identification." She writes concisely:

> Projective identification is bound up with developmental processes arising during the first three or four months of life (the paranoid-schizoid position) when splitting is at its height and persecutory anxiety predominates. The ego is still largely unintegrated and is therefore liable to split itself, its emotions and its internal and external objects, but splitting is also one of the fundamental defences against persecutory anxiety. Other defences arising at this stage are idealization, denial, and omnipotent control of internal and external objects. Identification by projection implies a combination of splitting off parts of the self

and projecting them on to (or rather into) another person. These processes have many ramifications and fundamentally influence object relations (Klein 1955, pp. 311–312).

In "On Identification" Klein also demonstrates projective identification through an interpretation of Julian Green's novel, *If I Were You*. It is the story of Fabian, a penniless, fatherless young man who resents his fate and makes a pact with the Devil to become someone else in order to claim the fortune he believes he deserves. In the course of many adventures he becomes a number of different people, taking over their identities. The advantages of being a rich man, a strong but stupid man, and even a handsome and healthy man soon wear thin; he is trapped within the limitations of each personality. But when he longs to become himself once again he is alienated from the memory of his name long since foresworn. When he is reconciled with the original Fabian, he longs for love, is overcome by a mysterious sense of happiness, and then dies. "As a result of overcoming the fundamental psychotic anxieties of infancy, the intrinsic need for integration comes out in full force," writes Klein of the novel's ending. Fabian "achieves integration concurrently with good object relations and thereby repairs what had gone wrong in his life" (p. 345).

Though Klein did not emphasize it in her interpretations, my own rereading of *If I Were You* compels me to mention the first stage in projective identification. Klein laid stress on the second stage, that of fusion with an other, but it is important to note the earlier step, that is, the basic quest for invisibility. Projective identification involves the desire of the infant—or the suffering adult—to become invisible, to disappear, or generally speaking, to negate one's own existence. Such phantasies of disappearing usually come at a high cost to self-esteem, the sense of authenticity, and self-connectedness. Patients who describe this phenomena believe that the body or soul that they have denied is no longer available to them for reparation.

My emphasis on the self-relationship involved in projective

identification, which owes lineage to the work of Bion (1970) and Kohut (1971, 1977), seeks to redress the balance which in Klein's work falls on the object relations aspects. It is important to remember that in projective identification there is a self left behind or disavowed, much as in *If I Were You* where Fabian's deserted self lies alone for three days in a coma.

A BASIC MECHANISM

Projective identification is an amalgam of concepts which can be confusing. When its purpose is defensive, projective identification aims really to *disavow* identification, and perhaps would be better called projective *dis*identification—the "I" wishes to split off some mental content, project it into an object, and then to sever any connection with itself. Moreover, like splitting, projective identification is both a benign defense which simply wishes to postpone confrontation with some experience that cannot yet be tolerated; but it is also a defense which can negate, destroy, and literally obliterate the sense of reality.

Before turning to the review of the literature, it will be useful to offer some guiding comments to orient projective identification both in terms of recent psychoanalytic theory and its historical genesis.

1. Projective identification is a schizoid mechanism, along with splitting, omnipotent denial, idealization, and introjection. These defenses are employed in the paranoid-schizoid position to defend against persecutory anxiety.

2. Splitting and projective identification work hand in hand. Generally speaking, projective identification acts as an adjunct to splitting by assigning a split-off percept or self to a container for postponement or for eradication. We can distinguish those aspects of projective identification which belong to the content of the mind from that aspect of the mind itself which wishes to disappear, become invisible, and negate its very existence. The defensive techniques which involve splitting off and projecting

mental content will result in states of mind different from those which seek to split off and project not only the content of experience but the capacity to experience the experience. The latter characterizes psychosis, borderline, narcissistic, and addictive disorders, etc.

As an instinctual vicissitude projective identification may be seen in three separate ways: *(a)* as the agent of the unpleasure principle, conducting the evacuation of painful accretion of stimuli from the self into an object; *(b)* as agent of the nirvana principle, seeking regressive dedifferentiation with the object of primary identification; and *(c)* as agent of magical omnipotent control.

3. Projection and projective identification are identical and interchangeable terms. There can be no projection without identification (or disidentification). The degree of splitting which attends the projection determines the degree to which it relies on disidentification of the self or reidentification of the self in the object, whether the object is intrapsychic or interpersonal.

I believe (Malin and Grotstein 1966) that in classical psychoanalytic thought an artifical distinction between projection and projective identification reflects a rigid distinction between the ego and the id, exposed by such authors as Fairbairn (1954), Gill (1963), Schur (1966), and Kohut (1971, 1977). On the other hand, Klein assumed, without fully realizing it, that the personality is integral and cannot be so easily separated into structural components as Freud suggested. Projection and projective identification suggest the translocation of aspects of self; a drive alone cannot be projected (as projection in the classical sense would suggest) without being reidentified in the object.

Wolheim (1969) has based a distinction between projection and projective identification on *(a)* the content of what is projected (mental qualities are projected and internal objects are projectively identified); and *(b)* the aim of the projections. With respect to the aim, Wolheim subtly distinguishes between the wish to remain in contact with the thought for reassurance that it is located in an external object (projection) and the wish to be rid of the thought and the internal object (projective identification as a state of thoughtlessness). While I believe that Wolheim is technically correct, my own psychoanalytic experience has convinced me that these distinctions fade in the clinical situation. "Mental qualities" is a way of talking about internal objects, and furthermore, the need for reassurance that a projection in an external object is only a denial of the identification implicit in the projection.

Langs (1976, 1978), Ogden (1978, 1979), Meissner (1980), and Ornston (1978a,b) have also attempted to distinguish between projection and projective identification, by relegating the former to an intrapsychic mechanism and conceiving of the latter as a transactional or bipersonal mechanism. While this seems to have some clinical validity, even "projection as a mental mechanism" involves projecting from a sense of "I" into the image of an external object for purposes of transactional or bipersonal manipulation. We do not project into objects in the external world; we project into our images of them. If our objects are in an intimate state of correspondence with us, they may be on a "shortwave" frequency and respond keenly to desires and wishes. (See 5, below)

4. All projection is identificatory to some extent. The very act of projection is a disavowal of identification in the first place; therefore, the basis of projection is a negative identification. Projection may formally establish identification with the object, but if not, then the object is believed to contain expelled identities which belong to the self despite the denial implicit in projection.

5. There can be no projective identification in a vacuum. The translocation of self or aspects of the self into an object always presupposes a preconception of an object which is a container. An object must be located via a primordial scanning, foraging, or exploration, and represents a primitive mechanism of normal thinking.

Bion (1958), as I stated earlier, has broadened our conception of projective identification by suggesting that the infant normally projects into a containing mother with reverie.* The infant's cries are urgent emotional communications which are experienced by mother as being projected into her with great momentum. "Reverie" refers to her receptivity (ability to be a "good enough" receptor site), in which her understanding and containment allow her to withstand the pain of projective urgency, sort it out, and act appropriately. This model, projection–containment–thoughtful action, constitutes the origins of normal thinking, and is normally internalized by the infant.

6. Projective identification invariably implies two separate states of anxiety: *(a)* the original anxiety which the experience of separation stimulates in the infant's or patient's mind; and *(b)* the anxiety which is the consequence of the employment of projective identification (e.g., claustrophobic anxiety or as a result of believing one is now trapped inside the substance or influence of an object).

7. I think it useful to think of *neurotic projective identification* as being experienced as an *extension* into an object hitherto believed to be separate, whereas *psychotic projective identification* is characterized by a *withdrawal* of the surviving self from the object and ego boundaries which formerly defined the self.

---

*I believe it is important to differentiate Bion's conception of containment from the mirroring mother as denoted by Lacan, Winnicott, and Kohut. Bion's "containment" is not so much an elastic or flexible impaction upon a silent maternal object as it is the mother's (and the analyst's) capacity to intercept the infant's inchoate communication (his organismic panic) and subject it to his or her own alpha function. Bion's conception is of an elaborated primary process activity which acts like a *prism* to refract the intense hue of the infant's screams into the components of the color spectrum, so to speak, so as to sort them out and relegate them to a hierarchy of importance and of mental action. Thus, containment for Bion is a very active process which involves feeling, thinking, organizing, and acting. Silence would be the least part of it. In psychoanalytic practice, the analyst uses a reverie corresponding to Bion's maternal reverie which allows for the entrance of the patient's projective identifications as countertransference or as projective counter-identifications, which can then be prismatically sorted out and lend themselves to effective understanding and ultimately to interpretations. In terms of the siamese twin paradigm, the bonding between the patient and the therapist constitutes the therapeutic alliance which allows for an umbilical-like "exchange transfusion."

The object and ego boundaries become confused with each other and become the transformed bizarre object of delusion and hallucinations.

A neurotic patient who recently began analysis, and who developed an idealizing transference to me, imagined me to be his extension—or conversely, he, mine. On the other hand, a schizophrenic patient in analysis, upon suffering a narcissistic injury, suddenly began to believe that the walls of my office had wire taps and that my phone was speaking to him. He also believed the FBI was after him. Subsequent analysis revealed that he experienced himself as having disappeared from his former self and the boundaries of that self. As he withdrew, he believed that I took over and was now in control of his former skin, sense organs, and mind (FBI). They were now alienated from him, possessed by me, and wanted to invade and control him.

8. Interpersonal projective identification must be distinguished from intrapsychic projective identification, although the two may overlap more than one would imagine. As I stated earlier, all projective identification is conducted into an internal object (self-object) or into an image of an external object (object representation). Thus, all projective identification is essentially intrapsychic. However, insofar as the boundary between the self and its objects is not completely defined, intrapsychic projective identification may be indistinguishable from interpersonal projective identification. In other words, they invariably are self-object transference phenomena. Thus, we can project into an object representation, but, in so doing, we transform the representation into an internal object (or self-object) unless the outside object optimally transforms the projection. One may also project into an already constituted internal object (self-object), making it a more complex entity. One may project, for instance, into a superego. Nevertheless, all projections, whether intrapsychic or interpersonal (whether into internal objects, self-objects, superego objects, or object representations) always involve disidentification from the self, reidentification in the object, and secondary identification with

the introjected transformation of that object which the projective identification has produced.

It must also be remembered that intrapsychic projection can be into separate psychic organizations, that is, split-off personalities within the psyche (split object representations). This is particularly true in psychotic, borderline, manic, and depressed patients who seem to utilize dissociated twin selves as targets for projection.

9. Splitting, as the agent of the principle of distinction or differentiation, and projective identification, as the agent of the principle of generalization, comprise the lowest common denominator of all defense mechanisms as well as of all perceptions and thought processes through varying differentiations, displacements, and secondary recombinations. Ultimately, repression, denial, isolation, doing-undoing, intellectualization, identification with the aggressor, etc., are combinations of splitting and projective identifications. Insofar as thinking and perception involves anticipation, selection, and reorganization of the gestalt or perception for mental storage, then splitting and projective identification are fundamentally involved in these processes. In this role splitting corresponds to differentiation, and projective identification corresponds to externalization insofar as it anticipates the perception.

10. Splitting and projective identification are not only mental mechanisms, they are also phantasies. Phantasy is the Rosetta Stone to all primitive communication and involves sensorimotor operations (Piaget 1952). The newborn infant "thinks" with its body, so that splitting and projective identification are enacted at a time before the body and the mind have made a clean differentiation. Projective identification is also involved in the formal thinking of adults, as the noun *project* cogently expresses. Thinking in adulthood is, after all, "trial action."

11. The phenomenon of transference, by and large, is one of projective identification with the aid of splitting. Oftentimes in analysis a person on the outside will receive the split-off transference from the analyst. Classical analysts generally believe that transference occurs as a displacement from a past object

cathexis to the analyst in the present. Although this is probably true, what is left out is that the infantile neurosis itself is a transference of the projective identifications of the infant's and child's self into his or her image of the parental object. The oedipus complex, for instance, is replete with multiple projective identifications of the child's phastasies about its parents. Thus, the transference neurosis is a displacement of past projective identifications.

Furthermore, transference occurs as a projective identification of aspects of the self in the present into or onto the figure of the analyst. Jacobson (1964) points out that object representations are displaceable but not projectable. Although this statement is correct, object representations (as well as self-representations) lose their representational status as soon as they are subject to projective identificatory transformation.

12. Projective identification, like splitting, has an epigenesis both zonally and in terms of object relations. Meltzer (1967) has described the sequence of the infant's projections into and from its oral, anal, and genital zones in relation to the breast, anus, genitals, and other organs of the object—and thereby establishes states of confusion between the zones of its own body and the parent's body. At the same time, projective identification can be seen to follow a sequence from autism, through symbiosis, to separation-individuation, including its four substages. I have already discussed autistic and symbiotic projective identification. In the depressive position of separation-individuation, however, projective identification is useful in establishing a particular kind of relationship to the object in which the object is also experienced as being a subject, just like the infant. The discovery of the object's subjectivity takes place in the rapprochement subphase and accounts for the development of empathy with the object, because the object is now felt to suffer feelings very much like the infant does.

13. Defensive projective identification involves the splitting-off and evacuation of *objects* of mind (feelings and thoughts), and the translocation of "I" or a portion of "I" (the *subject* of mind) into a transforming identification with an object. In

psychosis the mind itself is evacuated and "I" either disappears altogether or delusionally *becomes* the object (not just identified with the object). This "I" may even disclaim—or attempt to murder—the impostor who currently misrepresents him. Another feature of psychotic projective identification is the experience of telekinesis, in which the psychotic may projectively identify a split-off, disembodied twin self who is free to move about at will, leaving the body self abandoned.

14. Metathesis describes the imaginatively synthetic and recombinant aspects of creative projective identification and splitting. It can be demonstrated as follows. There are two solutions of chemicals, one containing sodium hydroxide (NaOH) and the other hydrochloric acid (HCl). The compounds may be split (constant conjection) into their respective moieties and recombined as NaCl and H_2O. Thus new compounds are created out of the original moieties. Metathesis is fundamental to the processes of dreamwork and creative imagination.

10

Freud on Projection

Freud's "Draft H," which he enclosed in an 1895 letter to Wilhelm Fliess, dealt with paranoia. "The purpose of paranoia," wrote Freud, "is thus to fend off an idea that is incompatible with the ego, by projecting its substance into the external world." It is a transposition (from internal to external) brought about by abuse of a normal psychic mechanism.

> Whenever an internal change occurs, we have the choice of assuming either an internal or an external cause. If something deters us from the internal derivation, we shall naturally seize upon the external one. Secondly, we are accustomed to our internal states being betrayed (by an expression of emotion) to other people. This accounts for normal delusions of observation and normal projection. For they are normal so long as, in the process, we remain conscious of our own internal change. If we forget it and we are left with only the leg of the syllogism that leads outwards, then there we have paranoia with its overvaluation of what people know about us and of what people have done to us. What do people know about us that we know nothing about, that we cannot admit? *It is, therefore, abuse of the mechanism of projection for purposes of defence.* (p. 209)

Freud also pointed out that, in contrast to states of hallucinatory confusion, in paranoia both the content and the affect are retained but "projected into the external world."

Drawing upon his 1895 formulations in "Draft H," in 1896 Freud published "Further Remarks on the Neuro-Psychoses of Defence," where he states concisely:

> In paranoia, the self-reproach is repressed in a manner which may be described as *projection*. It is repressed by erecting the defensive symptom of *distrust of other people*. In this way the subject withdraws his acknowledgement of the self-reproach; and, as if to make up for this, he is deprived of a protection against the self-reproaches which return in his delusional ideas. (p. 184)

THE SCHREBER CASE

Freud published his analysis of a case of paranoia in 1911, a study of the delusions of the jurist Daniel Paul Schreber as recounted in *Memoirs of My Mental Illness*. In this paper, Freud discussed projection with reference to at least two categories: one, a "secondary rationalization" insofar as Schreber's "miracled, cursorily improvised world" was the projection of his internal catastrophe; and the other use was as a psychotic form of repression. "It was incorrect to say that the perception which was suppressed internally is projected outwards; the truth is rather . . . that what was abolished internally returns from without" (p. 71).

Freud believed that Schreber's symptoms were, at bottom, due to homosexual libidinal impulses directed toward his physician (a famous neuropsychiatrist, Dr. Flechsig), ultimately a transference figure for his older brother. Freud's famous formulation of the paranoid transformation of love into hate and projection of persecutory phantasies is as follows.

> 'I (a man) love him' is contradicted by:
> Delusions of *persecution;* for they loudly assert:
> 'I do not *love* him—I *hate* him.'

The proposition that "I hate him" becomes transformed via projection:

'*He hates* (persecutes) *me,* which will justify me in hating him.'

And finally:

'I do not *love* him—I *hate* him, because HE PERSECUTES ME.' (p. 63)

TOTEM AND TABOO

Freud's 1912 essay on "some points of agreement between the mental lives of savages and neurotics" offers another discussion of projection, and for the first time hints at the normal use of projection in establishing the image of the external world. That is, Freud suggests that the external world is actually built up as projections of our perceptions and beliefs about our internal world.

The projection of unconscious hostility on to demons in the case of the taboo upon the dead is only a single instance of a number of the processes to which the greatest influence must be attributed in the shaping of the primitive mind. In the case we have been dealing with, projection served the purpose of dealing with an emotional conflict; and it is employed in the same way in a large number of psychic situations that lead to neuroses. But projection was not created for the purpose of defence; it also occurs where there is no conflict. The projection outwards of internal perceptions is a primitive mechanism, to which, for instance, our sense perceptions are subject, and which therefore normally plays a very large part in determining the form taken by our external world. Under conditions whose nature has not yet been sufficiently established, internal perceptions of emotional and thought processes can be projected outwards in the same way as sense perceptions; they are thus employed for building up the external world, though they should by rights remain part of the *internal* world. This may have some genetic connection with the fact that the function of attention was originally directed not towards the internal world but towards the stimuli that stream in from the external world, and that the function's only information upon endopsychic processes was received from feelings of pleasure and unpleasure. (p. 64)

This passage shows a cogent and decisive parallel between Freud's concept of projection with what would become Klein's concept of projective identification. That is, Freud substantiates Klein's idea that our image of the world is created via projective identification from sense impressions of the inner world. In a footnote Freud adds that "the projected creations of primitive man resemble the personifications constructed by creative writers; for the latter externalize in the form of separate individuals the opposing instinctual impulses struggling within them" (p. 65, n. 2). This again stresses the normal use of projection and would correspond to Klein's concept of benign or creative projective identification.

"Spirits and demons," writes Freud later in *Totem and Taboo,*

> . . . are only projections of man's own emotional impulses. He turns his emotional cathexes into persons, he peoples the world with them and meets his internal mental processes again outside himself—in just the same way as the intelligent paranoic, Schreber, found a reflection of the attachments and detachments of his libido in the vicissitudes of his confabulated 'rays of God'. (p. 92)

He goes on to say that projection will be used when it promises to bring mental relief, an advantage which can be expected when there is a conflict between different impulses, all of which are striving towards omnipotence—

> for they clearly cannot *all* become omnipotent. The pathological process in paranoia in fact makes use of the mechanism of projection in order to deal with mental conflicts of this kind. The typical case of such a conflict is one between the two members of a pair of opposites—the case of an ambivalent attitude, which we have examined . . . as it appears in someone mourning the death of a loved relative. This kind of case must seem particularly likely to provide a motive for the creation of projections. Here again we are in agreement with the writers who maintain that the first-born spirits were evil spirits, and who derive the idea of a soul from the impression made by death upon the survivors. (p. 92)

Freud lays stress here on the use of projection to resolve ambivalence; but his comments on the origin of evil spirits also suggest projective identification of the death instinct, as later elaborated by Klein.

PAPERS ON METAPSYCHOLOGY

In "Instincts and Their Vicissitudes" (1915a), Freud formalizes the mechanism of projection as counterpart to introjection—the latter associated with the libidinal instinct arising along the lines of the pleasure principle. Objects which are a source of unpleasure are expelled via projection.

> Thus the original 'reality-ego', which distinguished internal and external by means of a sound objective criterion, changes into a purified 'pleasure-ego', which places the characteristic of pleasure above all others. . . . It has separated off a part of its own self, which it projects into the external world and feels as hostile. After this new arrangement, the two polarities coincide once more: the ego-subject coincides with pleasure, and the external world with unpleasure (with what was earlier indifference). (p. 136)

Introjection and projection are two formal dispositions of instincts and, at the same time, the infant establishes a purified pleasure ego on the basis of the pleasure-unpleasure principle through a projection of bad or unwanted parts into the external world. Again, this formulation is in accord with Klein's (1957b) later conceptions of the origins of the external and internal world, and of projective identification.

In another of the metapsychological papers, "The Unconscious" (1915b), Freud details the use of projection in phobias and the general phobic disposition toward the source of anxiety—that is, the instinctual source is relocated from inside to outside as a perception via projection (projective identification).

> Further, we may lay stress on the interesting consideration that by means of the whole defensive mechanism thus set in action a

projection outward of the instinctual danger has been achieved. The ego behaves as if the danger of a development of anxiety threatened it not from the direction of an instinctual impulse but from the direction of a perception, and it is thus enabled to react against this external danger with the attempts at flight represented by phobic avoidances. (p. 184)

Freud emphasizes the use of projection in dreaming in "A Metapsychological Supplement to the Theory of Dreams" (1917a).

A dream tells us that something was going on which tended to interrupt sleep, and it enables us to understand in what way it has been possible to fend off this interruption. The final outcome is that the sleeper has dreamt and is able to go on sleeping; the internal demand which was striving to occupy him has been replaced by an external experience, whose demand has been disposed of. A dream is, therefore, among other things, a *projection:* an externalization of an internal process. (p. 223)

Later in the same paper Freud again stresses the more general importance of projection in the normal development of the sense of reality.

We [ascribe] to the still helpless organism the capacity for making a first orientation in the world by means of its perceptions, distinguishing 'external' and 'internal' according to their relation to its muscular action. A perception which is made to disapppear by an action makes no difference, the perception originates within the subject's own body—it is not real. It is of value to the individual to possess a means such as this of recognizing reality, which at the same time helps him to deal with it, and he would be glad to be equipped with a similar power against the often merciless claims of his intincts. That is why he takes such pains to transpose outwards what becomes troublesome to him from within—that is, to *project* it. (pp. 232-233)

Describing how the infant makes his instinctual internal reality into an external reality which is later introjected as a foreign world which invades the psyche, Freud suggests—I would infer—the notion of an id impulse errupting in the ego. This idea, which is how Freud defined the psychic apparatus, leaves open the question of whether the id is internal. I would suggest it is first projected, thereafter treated as extraterritorial to the sense of self, and later internalized.

LATER FORMULATIONS

In "The Uncanny" (1919) Freud deals with the phenomenon of the mysterious double, which he believes to be a remnant of the stage of primary narcissism and emerges as a projection of infantile omnipotence, executive of its disabuse by reality.

> The quality of uncanniness can only come from the fact of the 'double' being a creation dating back to a very early mental age, long since surmounted—a stage, incidentally, at which it wore a more friendly aspect. The "double" has become a thing of terror, just as, after the collapse of their religion, the gods turned into demons. (p. 236)

The sense of uncanniness comes about through projection of "material outward as something foreign to itself" (p. 236).

In discussing the origin of the "evil eye," Freud writes, "Whoever possesses something that is at once valuable and fragile is afraid of other people's envy, in so far as he projects onto them the envy he would have felt in their place" (p. 240). This more sophisticated use of envy is also suggestive of the Kleinian concepts—here, of projected transformations of envy and grief. In this regard, a similar discussion occurs in *Beyond the Pleasure Principle* (1920); Freud points out that a barrier or shield *(Reitschutz)* exists on the surface of the ego to protect it from external excitation, but that no such shield exists for internal processes. Therefore, the ego must project the impulses to the outside world and treat them as if they were external, so as, in phantasy, to subject them to the protective shield.

Melanie Klein must also have been interested by Freud's treatment of projected jealousy, analogous to projected envy, in

"Some Neurotic Mechanisms in Jealousy, Paranoia and Homosexuality" (1922). Projected jealousy, according to Freud,

> is derived in both men and women either from their own actual unfaithfulness in real life or from impulses towards it which have succumbed to repression. It is a matter of everyday experience that fidelity, especially that degree of it required in marriage, is only maintained in the face of continual temptations. Anyone who denies these temptations in himself will nevertheless feel the pressure so strongly that he will be glad enough to make use of an unconscious mechanism to alleviate his situation. He can obtain this alleviation—and, indeed, acquittal by his conscience—if he projects his own impulses to faithlessness on to the partner to whom he owes faith. . . .
> The jealousy that arises from such a projection has, it is true, an almost delusional character; it is, however, amenable to the analytic work of exposing the unconscious phantasies of the subject's own infidelity. (pp. 224–225)

A direct stimulus to Klein's development of the concept of projective identification, according to Jaques (1970), was Freud's treatment of the vicissitudes of identification in group processes in *Group Psychology and the Analysis of the Ego* (1921). He first pointed out that identification is the original form of emotional tie with an object and that, regressively, it can be a substitute for a libidinal object tie via introjection and assimilation. Most importantly, "it may arise with any new perception of a common quality shared with some other person who is not an object of the sexual instinct" (p. 108). Group formation involves a process in which each individual in the group thus identified with another surrenders his own ego-ideal and, through *idealization,* gives it over to the group leader.

The process of group formation, Freud points out, is similar to the phenomenon of hypnosis, in terms of the nature of the libidinal attachments. Identification is with the group members, and the object relationship, an idealized one, is coincident with the ego-ideal transposed to the leader or the hypnotist.

One can see here the projection of the ego-ideal into the

object. Where Freud emphasizes the identification between members of the group in contrast to the relationship to the ego-ideal, Klein would assume that the relationship to the leader is both an object relationship and an identification.

THE CONTRIBUTION OF TAUSK

Before turning to the work of Melanie Klein and her followers, it will be fruitful to examine how Victor Tausk applied Freud's concepts of projection and identification in his 1919 paper, "On the Origin of the 'Influencing Machine' in Schizophrenia." Tausk's paper—his first and last major contribution to psychoanalysis—shows him to have been alert to the enormous importance of the relationship between projection and identification, and to have sensed the importance of projective identification in the formation of normal and pathological structures within the ego.

Tausk writes of Miss Emma A., a paranoid who "maintained that her eyes were no longer properly placed in her head," that she

did not merely feel herself persecuted and influenced; hers was a case of the influence by *identification with* the persecutor. If we take into consideration the view held by Freud and myself that in object choice the mechanism of *identification* precedes the cathexis proper by *projection,* we may regard the case of Miss Emma A. as representing the stage in the development of the delusion of reference preceding the projection (namely, on to a distant persecutor in the outer world). The identification is obviously an attempt to project the feelings of the inner change on to the external world. (p. 58; my italics)

Later in the paper, describing the formation of the influencing machine in a psychotic patient, Tausk states:

It [the machine] represents the projection of the patient's body on to the outer world. At least, the following results are unquestionably obtained from the patient's report: the apparatus is distinguished above all by its human form, easily recognized despite many non-human characteristics. In form it resembles the patient herself, as she senses all manipulations performed on the apparatus in the corresponding part of her own body and in the same manner. All effects and changes undergone by the apparatus take place simultaneously in the patient's body and *vice versa*. Thus, the apparatus loses its genitalia following the patient's loss of her genital sensations. (p. 64)

Tausk clearly delineates the intimate relationship between projection and identification. The influencing machine is a projection of the patient's body parts into external space, presumably into an idea of an external object. Nevertheless—despite the projection—the identification with the projected parts remains intact in the mind of the patient: an effect in one part is felt simultaneously in the other. (As I hope to show later, this aspect of identification in projection is due either to an absence of splitting or denial or to ineffective splitting or denial, so that the persistence of the connection in the projection remains.)

Tausk evolves the theme that the development of the infantile ego is due to a projection of one's body parts and subsequent identification with them.

The projection of one's body may, then, be traced back to the developmental stage in which one's body is the goal of object finding. This must be the time when the infant is discovering his body, part by part, as the outer world, and is still groping for his hands and feet as though they were foreign objects. At this time, everything that "happens" to him emanates from his own body; his psyche is the object of stimuli arising in his own body but acting upon it as if produced by outer objects. These disjecta membra are later on pieced together and systematized into a unified whole under the supervision of a psychic unity that receives all sensations of pleasure and pain from these separate parts. This process takes place by means of identification with one's own body. . . .

But if the psycho-analytic theories previously employed are correct, this object finding within one's own organs, which can be regarded as parts of the outer world only by projection, must be preceded by a stage of identification with a narcissistic libidio position, and it is necesssary to assume two successive stages of identification and projection.

The projection which participated in the object finding within one's own organs would, then, be the second phase of the preceding stage, although the part that depends upon the postulated identification has still to be discoverd.

I am, then, assuming the existence of these two successive phases of *identification* and *projection* in object finding and object choice within one's own body. (pp. 72-73; my italics)

In essence, Tausk is pointing out that *(a)* the self is the ego's first object and is discovered in two stages of projective indentification, the first of which is the projection of one aspect of the ego in a state of primary identification outward onto a body part; and *(b)* once this projection of ego into its body part-object-self has been established, it is secondarily identified with and accepted as part of the ego. Further, this double process of projective identification and subsequent reintrojection is a pattern of normal development.

In psychosis, Tausk also suggests, projection (projective identification) does *not* take place because the very ego boundaries which are laid down through normal projective identification dissolve. What appear as projections are the residua of the sense organs which belong to the former periphery of the body ego confronting an ego which is withdrawing into a constricted center. Hallucinations represent the residue of the self at its former frontier, confronting a gap from which the sense organs have been alienated. *What seems to be projection really is the shrinking of an ego.*

11

The Kleinian Contribution

The general Kleinian usage of projective identification has been set out by Segal (1964).

> From the original projection of the death instinct there evolves another mechanism of defence, extremely important in [the paranoid-schizoid position], namely, projective identification. In projective identification parts of the self and internal objects are split off and projected into the external object, which then become possessed by, controlled and identified with the projected parts.
>
> Projective identification has manifold aims: it may be directed toward the ideal object to avoid separation, or it may be directed toward the bad object to gain control of the source of danger. Various parts of the self may be projected, with various aims: bad parts of the self may be projected in order to get rid of them as well as to attack and destroy the object, good parts may be projected to avoid separation or to keep them safe from bad things inside or to improve the external object through a kind of primitive projective reparation. Projective identification starts when the paranoid-schizoid position is first established in relation to the breast, but it persists and very often becomes intensified when the mother is perceived as a whole object and the whole of her body is entered by projective identification. (pp. 27–28)

Although projective identification was not named as such

until Melanie Klein's first detailed description of the first three months of life, "Notes on Some Schizoid Mechanisms" (1946), the lineage of the concept can be traced through her earliest papers. As noted in chapter 3, the process of splitting was suggested in "The Development of a Child" (1921); in the same paper Klein also made use of projection. Discussing splitting and projection in relation to her original account of transference, in "Personification in the Play of Children" (1929), she regarded these mechanisms as a means of displacing conflict into the external world and consequent diminished anxiety. "In schizophrenia," she added, "in my opinion, the capacity for personification and for transference fails, amongst other reasons, through the defective functioning of the projection-mechanism. This interferes with the capacity for establishing or maintaining the relation to reality and the external world" (p. 224). Here emphasizing the importance of the capacity for personification and the importance of phantasy as prerequisite for transference, I believe she also first adumbrated her later theory of projective identification and intuitively laid the foundations for the concept of defective projection in schizophrenia.

EARLY STAGES OF THE OEDIPUS CONFLICT AND OF SUPER-EGO FORMATION

In chapter 8 of *The Psycho-Analysis of Children*, Melanie Klein (1932) discussed the concomitant formation of the super-ego and oedipus impulses, which she dated as beginning in the middle of the first year of life. In this anal-sadistic stage, wrote Klein, the infant's

> methods of defence are violent in the extreme, since they are proportionate to the excessive pressure of anxiety. We know that in the early anal-sadistic stage what he is ejecting is his object, which he perceives as something hostile to him and which he equates with excrement. In my view, what is already being ejected . . . is his terrifying super-ego which he has introjected in the oral-sadistic stage of his development. Thus his act of ejection is a means of defence employed by his fear-ridden ego

against his super-ego; it expels his internalized objects and projects them into the outer world. The mechanisms of projection and expulsion in the individual are closely bound up with the process of super-ego formation. (pp. 140-141)

Whereas previously she had considered projection in terms of the libidinal and aggressive instincts, and of phantasied internal objects as impulses or portions of the psychic apparatus, in this paper internal objects are sophisticated self-constructed phantoms occupying mental space and projection is a mechanism for their riddance.

Later in the same chapter Klein discusses the reciprocity between introjection and projection in personality development, in a way which hints at a link between projection and identification in the formation of psychic structure.

The fact that the image of his objects is distorted by the individual's own sadistic impulses has the following consequences: it not only puts a different complexion on the influence exerted by real objects and by his relations to them, on the formation of his super-ego, but . . . also increases the importance of his super-ego in regard to his object-relations. When, as a small child, he first begins to introject his objects—and these, it must be remembered, are yet only very vaguely demarcated by his various organs—his fear of those introjected objects sets in motion the mechanisms of ejection and projection, as I have tried to show; and there now follows a reciprocal action between projection and introjection, which seems to be of fundamental importance not only for the formation of his super-ego but for the development of his object relations and his adaptation to reality. The steady and continual urge he is under *to project his terrifying identifications* onto his objects results, it would seem, in an increased impulse to repeat the process of introjection again and again, and is thus itself a decisive factor in the evolution of his relationship to objects. (pp. 142-143; italics mine)

Finally, Klein also delineates the ultimate nature of the early formation of the personality, that is, through the synchronized interaction of projection and introjection—a projection of terrifying images into the external world and introjection of good images. In this sense her concept is parallel to Freud's idea of the formation of a purified pleasure ego. Klein writes:

> The interaction between super-ego formation and object-relation, based on an interaction between projection and introjection, profoundly influences his development. In the early stages, the projection of his terrifying images into the external world turns that world into a place of danger and his objects into enemies; while the simultaneous introjections of real objects which are in fact well-disposed to him, works in the opposite direction and lessens the force of his fear of the terrifying images. Viewed in this light, super-ego formation, object-relations and adaptation to reality are the result of an interaction betwen the projection of the individual's sadistic impulses and the introjection of his objects. (p. 148)

SOME THEORETICAL CONCLUSIONS REGARDING THE EMOTIONAL LIFE OF THE INFANT

Projective identification as distinct from projection was first described by Klein in this paper, delivered as part of the Controversial Discussions before the British Psycho-Analytical Society in 1943–1944, but not published until 1952. Discussing the role of projection in persecutory anxiety, she wrote:

> Attacks derived from all other sources of sadism soon become linked with these oral attacks [phantasies of devouring and scooping out the mother's body] and two main lines of sadistic phantasies develop. One form—mainly oral-sadistic and bound up with greed—is to empty the mother's body of everything good and desirable. The other form of phantasied attack—predominantly anal—is to fill her body with bad substances and parts of the self which are split off and projected into her. These are mainly represented by excrements which become the means of damaging, destroying or controlling the attacked object. Or the whole self—felt to be the 'bad' self—enters the mother's body and takes control of it. In these various phantasies, the ego takes

possession by projection of an external object—first of all the mother—and makes it into an extension of the self. The object becomes to some extent a representative of the ego, and these processes are in my view the basis for identification by projection or 'projective identification'. Identification by introjection and identification by projection appear to be complementary processes. It seems that the processes underlying projective identification operate already in the earliest relation to the breast. . . . Accordingly, projective identification would start simultaneously with the greedy oral-sadistic introjection to the breast. (pp. 206–207)

This passage formally states the hypothesis of projective identification for the first time, by which Klein suggests a sophisticated or enhanced process of projection whose mechanism not merely rids the ego of unwanted stimuli or bad objects, but also extends into and takes possession of an object.

NOTES ON SOME SCHIZOID MECHANISMS

A major theoretical contribution in which Klein describes the paranoid-schizoid position (as she renamed the paranoid position), she elaborates projective identification, now born as a concept which bridges the gap between projection as a mental mechanism and identification as a primitive object relationship. And it is clear that it is a mechanism with far-reaching consequences for pathology. Projection of split-off parts of the ego "are meant not only to injure but also to control and to take possession of the object," wrote Klein. "In so far as the mother comes to contain the bad parts of the self, she is not felt to be a separate individual but is felt to be *the* bad self."

Much of the hatred against parts of the self is now directed towards the mother. This leads to a particular form of identification which establishes the prototype of an aggressive object-relation. I suggest for these processes the term 'projective identification'. When projection is mainly derived from the infant's impulse to harm or to control the mother, he feels her to be a persecutor. In psychotic disorders the identification of an object with the hated parts of the self contributes to the intensity of the hatred directed against other people. . . .

It is, however, not only the bad parts of the self which are expelled and projected, but also good parts of the self. . . . The identification based in this type of projection vitally influences object-relations. The projection of good feelings and good parts of the self into the mother is essential for the infant's ability to develop good object-relations and to integrate his ego. However, if this projective process is carried out excessively, good parts of the personality are felt to be lost, and in this way the mother becomes the ego-ideal; this process too results in weakening and impoverishing the ego. (pp. 300–301)

And a weakened ego "becomes also incapable of assimilating its internal objects, and this leads to the feeling that it is ruled by them."

In terms of later pathology, projective identification

is at the basis of many anxiety-situations, of which I shall mention a few. The phantasy of forcefully entering the object gives rise to the dangers threatening the subject from within the object. For instance, the impulses to control an object from within it stir up the fear of being controlled and persecuted inside it. By introjecting and re-introjecting the forcefully entered object, the subject's feelings of inner persecution are strongly reinforced; all the more since the re-introjected object is felt to contain dangerous aspects of the self. The accumulation of anxieties of this nature, in which the ego is, as it were, caught between a variety of external and internal persecution-situations, is a basic element in paranoia.

I have previously described [in "Early Stages of the Oedipus Conflict and of Super-ego Formation," discussed above] the infant's phantasies of attacking and sadistically entering the mother's body as giving rise to various anxiety-situations (particularly the fear of being imprisoned and persecuted within her) which are at the bottom of paranoia. I also showed that the fear of being imprisoned (and especially of the penis being attacked) inside the mother is an important factor in later disturbances of male potency (impotence) and also underlies claustrophobia. (p. 305)

ON IDENTIFICATION

Primarily an analysis of the novel by Julian Green, *Fabian,* which I discussed earlier in chapter 6, in "On Identification," Klein made two points with respect to the concept of projective identification as described in "Schizoid Mechanisms" which deserve mention. One of them concerns her idea that the projection of good parts of the self was essential to integration and competent object relationships; she now added "that a securely established good object, implying a securely established love for it, gives the ego a feeling of riches and abundance which allows for an outpouring of libido and projection of good parts of the self into the external world without a sense of depletion arising" (p. 312).

Klein also adds to her discussion of projective identification with respect to anxiety situations, quoted at the conclusion of the previous section, above. There she had suggested that the fear of being imprisoned within the mother's body related, in subsequent pathology, to claustrophobia. "I would now add," she writes, "that projective identification may result in the fear that the lost part of the self will never be recovered because it is buried in the object." (p. 337)

BION'S DEVELOPMENT OF THE CONCEPT

In her later works, *Envy and Gratitude* (1957) and *Narrative of a Child Analysis* (1960), Klein maintained the concept of projective identification which she had detailed in "Notes on Some Schizoid Mechanisms" and elaborated in "On Identification." But it has been explored by many other psychoanalysts besides Melanie Klein, and although space does not permit a proper examination of every contribution, the work of Bion is particularly interesting, not too well known, and suggests the ultimate importance of projective identification in both pathological and normal phenomena.

Since the writings of Tausk, which were discussed in the last chapter, explorations of projective identification have often been made by analysts whose major clinical interest is in schizophrenia and allied conditions. Rosenfeld, for example, has discussed projective identification extensively in the papers comprising his *Psychotic States* (1965), and in his opinion it is the most important element for technique in treating these conditions. His paper, "Notes on the Psychopathology and Psychoanalytic Treatment of Schizophrenia," furthermore illustrates the way in which Kleinian workers have employed projective identification as a tactical innovation, that is, how they use it to explain how the schizophrenic invades the object with his violent feelings, transforms the object by virtue of this invasion into destroying and destroyed objects, then identifies with both.

Like Rosenfeld, Bion makes projective identification a key to understanding psychosis. "I do not think real progress with psychotic patients is likely to take place," he writes,

> until due weight is given to the nature of the divergence between the psychotic and non-psychotic personality, and in particular the role of projective identification in the psychotic part of the personality as a substitute for regression in the neurotic part of the personality. The patient's destructive attacks on his ego and the substitution of projective identification of a repression and introjection must be worked through. (1957, p. 63)

Or, as he states elsewhere (1956), "Projective identification of conscious awareness and the associated inchoation of verbal thought is the central factor in the differentiation of the psychotic from the non-psychotic personality" (p. 38). Massive resort to projective identification in schizophrenia depends, Bion believes, on the following four features: (1) conflict between life and death instincts with a (2) preponderance of destructive impulses; (3) a hatred of external and internal reality and (4) a tenuous but tenacious object relationship. Projective identification is directed against the apparatus of perception and causes it to be split up into fragments and sent off into objects. An associated phenomenon is the psychotic's inability to introject. If he wishes to take in an interpretation, or bring back these objects I have been describing, he does so by projective identification reversed. . . . I would now add that, thanks to this employment of projective identification, he cannot synthesize his objects: he can only agglomerate and compress them. . . . It will be clear that where the non-psychotic personality, or part of the personality, employs repression the psychotic has employed projective identification. . . .

Further, excessive projective identification in the paranoid-schizoid position prevented smooth introjection and assimilation of sense impressions and consequently the establishment of the firm base of good objects on which the inception of verbal thought depends. . . .

An attempt to think involves bringing back to control, and therefore to his personality, the expelled particles and their accretions. Projective identification is therefore reversed and the concomitant agglomeration and compression lead to highly compact speech, the construction of which is more appropriate to music than the articulation of words as used for non-psychotic communication. (pp. 40–41)

In several other papers collected in *Second Thoughts* (1967), Bion explores aspects of projective identification in schizophrenia. "On Arrogance" (1957b) concerns the formation of what Bion calls the "obstructive object." He believes that there is a triad of symptoms: arrogance, stupidity, and curiosity, which occur in schizophrenics quite commonly, due to a series of primeval events in the life of an infant who projects his fear of dying into a mother whose capacity for reverie is deficient. As a consequence of her deficiency, the infant develops the phantasy of a destroyed or defective mother, with whom he identifies on one level, and also an obstructive mother who purposefully refuses to contain his projections. At the same time his dangerous curiosity has been transformed and becomes the arrogance of stupidity rather than the arrogance of curiosity, and is characterized by massive projective identification of all awarenesses or accretions of awareness from the psyche. This is the first paper in which Bion invoked the transactional conception into Kleinian metapsychology and assigned to the mother with reverie responsibility for at least fifty percent of the interaction. This paper undoubtedly was the birthplace for his later concept of the container and the contained. At the same time he seems to indicate that projective identification is the forerunner of normal communication between infant and mother.

In his 1958 paper, "On Hallucination," Bion suggests as the first step toward understanding hallucinatory phenomena:

> if the patient says he sees an object it may mean an external object has been perceived by him or it may mean that he is ejecting an object through his eyes. If he says he hears something it may mean he is ejecting a sound—this is *not* the same thing as making a noise: if he says he feels something it may mean tactile sensation is being extruded, thrown off by his skin. An awareness of the double meaning that verbs of sense have for the psychotic sometimes makes it possible to detect an hallucinatory process before it betrays itself by more familiar signs. (p. 67)

The psychotic patients Bion was studying had invariably projected bad aspects of themselves into him, therefore imagined him to be bad or persecutory, then ingested those same aspects, and finally projected them into space via the sense organs. There would be a crossover: for instance, the patient would take in something bad from the ears and project it out with the eyes. Interpretations were taken in and ejected this way.

Similarly, a dream for the psychotic is an "evacuation of material that has been taken in during waking hours" (p. 78). Psychotic dreams by day and by night are really hallucinations, and are massive projective indentifications of and from the sense organs so as to rid the psyche of the accretions of stimuli which would otherwise disturb the patient. The psychotic projects not only thoughts but also the sense organs and the mind which receives the thoughts and feelings. Hallucinations will contain some element of mind and sense organ.

In "A Theory of Thinking" Bion (1962a) elaborates the relationship between normal projective identification and what he names "alpha function," which accounts for any and all of the transformations of sense impressions into mental elements suitable for storage by the mind. (Alpha function is similar to primary process but is more sophisticated. Bion later provided a "grid" which suggests the alpha function transformations of sense impressions into thought.) The model of the infant-mother reverie as "thought couple" establishes a paradigm for projective identification by an infantile self into a mother container, with which the growing infant may be identified as receptor for his projections, as a model for thinking. Projective identification can therefore be thought of as the conduit for the id into the ego, and from both into the superego. It therefore is closely associated (identified) with instinctual force or psychic energy.

The explanation of the genesis of normal thinking as projective identification of impulses and sensations into a mother with reverie inaugurated a new trend in Bion's thinking, which had previously been much in keeping with contemporary Kleinian theory. From his 1962 book, *Learning From Experience,* Bion's notion of instincts has involved the duality of sense impressions and inherent preconceptions (instinctual knowledge)—both subject to alpha function for storage as memory or for thinking and mental action. Projective identification, consequently, becomes the vehicle for the relay of sense impressions or inherent preconceptions to the surface of the mind as "thoughts without a thinker." Therefore, in terms of psychotic states, Bion refers to excessive projective identification:

> The patient's ability to gear his omnipotent phantasy of projective identification to reality is directly related to his capacity for tolerence of frustration. If he cannot tolerate frustration the omnipotent phantasy of projective identification has proportionately less factual counterpart in external reality. This contributes to the state Melanie Klien describes as *excessive* projective identification. The excess however must be scrutinized carefully. It may appear to be excessive because the analyst is forced to be aware of it by the realistic steps which the patient takes to make the analyst in fact experience emotions of a

kind the patient does not want to have (M. Klein). *This* excess must be sharply distinguished from the excessive projective identification which represents a resort to omnipotent phantasy as a flight from reality, and in particular from feelings which are not wanted. But projective identification cannot exist without its reciprocal, namely an introjective activity intended to lead to an accumulation of good internal objects. (1962b, p. 32)

Finally, Bion added yet another dimension to projective identification in *Experience in Groups* (1959b), a book which parallels Freud's concepts in *Group Psychology and the Analysis of the Ego* (1921). Bion points out that when members of a group focus on a common purpose, they relate to each other and also relate to the leader of the group. Using the classical analytic approach, Bion realized that by not yielding to the pressure to become the group ideal, as Freud realized, certain frictional elements would begin to evolve in the group's psychology. For instance, the group would seem to divide, side by side with its unity for the work purpose, into subgroups or "basic assumption groups." These basic assumption groups are of three main categories: the basic assumption group of dependence, the basic assumption group of pairing, and the basic assumption group of fight-flight. In this situation there are several forms of identification and projection going on. In particular, there is a normal aspect of transitory or temporary identification in terms of the unification of the group to perform the common focus or purpose. There are then subsidiary identifications of a more pathological kind when friction begins to develop, insofar as these basic assumption groups involve different members in which each member of each group is identified with each other on the basis of a pathological premise and all have projected aspects of themselves, individually and in common, into members of other basic assumption groups. The latter constitutes a form of projective identification.

In short, Bion's thesis is that if the group leader refuses to accept the projective identification of the hypnotic idealization from each and all members of the group, then a process ensues in which the inherent tendency towards projection onto a leader will have secondary splitting ramifications which will involve projective and identificatory processes.

Bion's progressive concern with development of projective identification is both important unto itself and significant as an example of the expanding range of the concept. Klein and her followers thought of projective identification as a schizoid defense which furthered the work of splitting and which comprised magic omnipotent denial and idealization. They first regarded it as instrumental in states of confusion between the infantile self and its objects, instigated in order to ward off the awareness of separation. As such, its main usage by Kleinian writers was originally as an early object relationship. Bion (and Rosenfeld) clarified the nature of abnormal projective identification in psychotic states. Later, Bion recognized that projective identification was also the basic and inchoate instigator of thinking insofar as the projective identifications from an infant into the container mother is the model for all future thought (the model of the "thinking couple").

OTHER CONTRIBUTIONS

Apart from Freud and Tausk, some of the early first or second generation analysts to discuss projective identification include Feigenbaum (1936), Nunberg (1920, 1921), and Paul Federn and his student, Edoardo Weiss. Federn (1952), in his important contribution to our understanding of the psychoses, suggested that true projection was due to a loss of ego boundary cathexis, a conception which I find congruent with my own understanding. Weiss noticed as early as 1947 that projection and identification were often confused with one another, and developed the intriguing idea of an "extraject," a meaningful operational distinction that serves to emphasize how projection falsifies data in the external world. Finally, as is well known, Anna Freud discussed aspects of projection in *The Ego and the Mechanisms of Defence* (1936), particularly in the chapter, "A Form of Altruism," and also in terms of "identification with the aggressor."

Among Kleinians, Hanna Segal (1964) and Paula Heimann (1952) have clarified the original concept, and Elliot Jaques (1970) has applied it to social interaction. At the beginning of this chapter I mentioned that Rosenfeld had applied the formulations of projective identification to the study of psychotic states (1965); a definitive treatise he has written (1971) also deserves mention: "Contribution to the Psychopathology of Psychotic States: The Importance of Projective Identification in the Ego Structure and the Object Relations of the Psychotic Patient." He compares his views with those of Klein, and also discusses the clinical and critical contributions of the late Edith Jacobson.

In chapter 4, Kernberg's considerations of splitting were discussed in a little detail. He has also studied projective identification (1975), and distinguished it from projection. In all, however, his conception of projective identification corresponds to Kleinian thinking exactly. He has added certain metapsychological modifications introduced by Fairbairn (see chapter 4), and also added the Freudian concept of drive.

In volume 7 of the *International Journal of Psychoanalytic Psychotherapy,* Ogden (1978) and Ornston (1978a) have both discussed projective identification; and the latter has also conducted a noteworthy and diligent review of Freud's use of projection (1978b). With a viewpoint which differs from the one presented in this book, Ogden (1979) has attempted to set out rigorous criteria for distinguishing projection from projective identification, as has Meissner (1980).

Heinrich Racker (1968) and Leon Grinberg (1962) have discussed the relationship of projective identification to countertransference and the analytic process. From a classically-based but unique position, Searles (1959) has described a form of projective identification in a treatment context which he calls *symbiotic relatedness.*

Space does not permit a longer discussion of all the above papers, and many others besides, among them: Sarnoff's 1972 paper on projection during adolescence, Wangh's (1962) "The 'Evocation of a Proxy,'" Meltzer's work drawn from his work with autistic children (1967), and Lang's (1976) discussion in terms of his concept of the bipersonal field. Other important papers include Malin and Grotstein (1966), Smith (1974), Novick and Kelly (1970), and Berg (1977).

12

Splitting and Projective Identification in Psychoanalytic Therapy

1. Psychopathology and mental health emerge as the more nearly permanent structures which have been appended onto the scaffolding erected by imagination. Imagination is the experience of projective identification and splitting; and psychopathology can be thought of as the misadventure of imagination, precociously foreclosed upon, or caught in a time warp and carried forward intact. As instruments of imagination, splitting and projective identification help us decipher pathology by locating it in its time warp and comprehending its unique imaginative semiotic. Psychoanalytic psychotherapy is imagination in reverse.

2. In the course of analysis the patient externalizes his imaginative inner world onto the psychoanalytic screen for explication. As the therapy deepens, transference takes place in which the analyst is projectively identified with assignments of various roles from the patient's inner world. The transference may be split between good and bad, idealized and evil, etc.; and the patient may seek to involve the analyst in infantilistic combinations concerning the zones of his or her body and phantasies about the "geography" of the analyst's body. For example, the patient may wish to evade the anxieties of separation (envy, for instance) by oral invasion of mother's breast (analyst's mind), either directly or perversely, through the anus

or genital. As the projective identification continues to elaborate, splitting between self and self, object and object, and self and object proliferate. The development of resistance *pari passu* with development of the transference often indicates the patient's attempt to defend himself against claustrophobic anxiety consequent upon his fear of being taken over by the analyst into whom he has projected his needy self. It thus represents a repetition of the development of a boundary between self and object alongside the transaction of need between self and object as a guarantee of separateness.

3. Psychoanalytic psychotherapy is characterized from the very beginning by assignment of both the therapeutic alliance and container capacity to the analyst and to the analysis, following which there is a continuous interplay between externalizing free association and defensive splitting and projective identification. The analyst is alert to the patient's repetition of his developmental tendency to confuse his zones and the analyst's zones and, through interpretations, the analyst helps the patient to restore the normal boundaries (neutralized "splitting" or differentiation) between them, as well as the sorting out (making new distinctions) between previous misconceptions.

In the normal course of performing analysis, the analyst must collect the disparate, disconnected free associations of the patient's language of experience—*and* the feelings which are implicit and explicit to them—and then subject them to the grammer of his or her own language of achievement. The employment of this language requires consummate patience, intuition, empathy, and synthetic and recombinative imagination, which are sublimated forms of splitting and projective identification.

4. Of particular importance is the phenomenon of the split transference in which the analyst seems to represent one aspect of an internal object, and an object or objects on the outside represent other split-off aspects. It is very important to "gather the transference," as Meltzer (1967) advises. Otherwise, the

analysis exists in a split-off, polarized state and never seems to emerge from a paranoid solution to the patient's problem. From the standpoint of the archaic, infantile transference situation, Kleinian workers find it useful to consider all the objects in the patient's day residue as vicissitudes of aspects of the self or of the analyst/mother. In the strictest sense it conforms to the conception of the relationship of the zones of the infant's body to the geography of the mother's body. On another level the objects in the patient's day residue are important in their own right and must also be considered from that standpoint since they occupy the scene of the patient's concentration of emotions. Yet the therapeutic discipline of considering all objects and situations as vicissitudes of the transference, whether interpreted or not, offers the patient the security of being shepherded into a primitive transference neurosis which gathers the transference from all the split-off and projected feelings which have been exiled into the diaspora of the patient's daily external world. The proper gathering of the transference thereby allows a more nearly complete working through of the patient's infantile neurosis.

5. The split transference is but the flip side of the revelation of multiple splits in the patient's personality which become unraveled in the analytic situation. As I have stated over and over again, it is my impression that impulses which emerge from other than a cohesive self denote splittings of the personality into entities which are like split-off whole personalities. Every ego-dystonic impulse emerges, I believe, from an alien self which has long ago sequestered itself within the framework of the overall personality and has continued to live under a repression which keeps the cohesive self from recognizing it. When repression is lessened , for whatever reason, the splits in the self seem to emerge much more clearly as, for instance, in borderline and psychotic illness. These splits may either be highly polarized as in manic-depressive borderline states, or amorphous and fragmentary as in schizoid borderline states.

6. The purpose of the analysis is to allow the splits to define themselves so that their nature can be known and a rapprochement between them be achieved in the reconciliatory state of at-one-ment. Macroscopic and microscopic splits of the personality which have not been integrated into the forward sweep of the cohesive momentum of the personality exist, instead, in split-off independent states. They seem to be enclosed in nefarious dungeons and time warps and seek to become integrated with the rest of the personality by perforating the precocious closure which in the past has separated them off from the rest of the personality. It is no exaggeration to state that splits of the personality constitute the return of the repressed and are the efforts of split-off selves to return to the personality. In therapy, here again empathy is the issue of utmost importance. Not only must the analyst be empathic towards the patient, as Kohut emphasizes, but the analyst must through his interpretations, according to Bion, enjoin the patient to empathize with those split-off aspects of himself from which he long ago withdrew. Thus, the goal of analysis is to promote the patient's empathy towards his splits and thereby diminish his antipathy contained within the split objects themselves and the splitting which predicates the antipathy.

In other contributions (Grotstein, 1979d, f) I have employed the paradigm of demoniacal possession to include those aspects of the self which have been split-off and projectively identified into a negative ego-ideal and then secondarily demonized as perpetually profane. I believe this to be a model for all psychopathology. It is a theory which includes both nature and nurture. If a parent is antipathetic, one can projectively identify with the parent on one hand, and disavow that aspect of oneself on the other by reassigning it to an imagined profane object. Demoniacal possession, then, is a way of talking about the enfeebled and embattled self which turns against itself and disavows those aspects which it believes it can no longer bear. The self now identifies with the intimidating object and disavows those aspects of itself which it now dislikes and sends them into either repression/or denial. By repression, I mean taking away its name (decathexis) and renaming it in mythical terms (instinctualization by dreaming or by phantasy-formation so as to render it alienated, mystified, and my-thified). This aspect of the self therefore loses its original name and attains a false new name—but one which is unknown to the disavowing self.

In denial not only is the name taken away, but the object is sent into oblivion. Its ghost returns as nameless dread. It is of very great importance for the principle of empathy to be applied by the analyst and by the patient to the split-off selves, including evil aspects of the self. All aspects of the self which are not part of the normal cohesive self are split-off selves which have undergone traumatic disavowal and seek return and admittance so as to re-achieve at-one-ment. Thus, affects and symptoms are but highly disguised, friendly warnings of lost selves seeking to rejoin us. Hartmann, Erikson, Bion, and Kohut help us to see through the adaptational principle that whenever we use an instinctual mode of splitting or projective identification, we do it because we are caught in a state of abject helplessness and seek a moment's sanctuary in order to survive. Psycho-pathology is the price of that survival and also the interest on the loan of a security which allows us to survive by disavowing aspects of ourselves—nonetheless destined to return with al-tered names or with no names so as to be re-cognized and allowed re-entry. Splitting and projective identification are the tools of this reunion as well as the tools of the original dis-avowal and exodus.

A patient who is in the motion picture industry mentioned that, upon his first and subsequent successes on stage and on the screen, he experienced a feeling of emptiness. While discussing his present problems of financial overextension, he stated that he wanted to "disappear." I had heard him say that on previous occasions, but this time I was able to link his tendency to disappear with his low sense of self-esteem and with his conse-quent inability to face problems. His form of disappearance was either a psychical one, in which case he seemingly projectively identified himself with an idealized image of his own father or of other father figures, or he would disappear geographically by retreating to the mountains and fantasying himself a powerful medieval baron. The escape identities were projective identifications into powerful figures, the identifications with whom gave him the feeling of safety. On the other hand, the self left behind (which he designated by a slightly different first name) was experienced as contemptibly derelict. However, when he achieved success, it was empty because, believing that he had forfeited his identity, he had also forfeited the right to accept the rewards of success. "Success is not in my scenario," he would state. "If it comes, it is by mistake and must be given back."

This is an example of projective identification of the self into an internalized object (an idealized object) and therefore constitutes an intrapsychic projective identification consequent to the splitting. This idealized object was a combination of his image of his ego ideal in addition to an omnipotent, maniacal self, as Rosenfeld and Kernberg have pointed out to be true in narcissistic cases. In addition, most important for the treatment was being able to show the patient that he was projectively identified with an idealized image of a tyrannical father and of an abandoning mother, both of whom were experienced by him in actual life as having withdrawn from him during his infancy, childhood, and young adulthood. His power was therefore located in being identified with powerful objects who withdrew from him, so his withdrawal from himself in the act of disappearance was siding with them against himself. The treatment of this situation involved identifying the projective identifications and the splits of self, gathering them, unifying them, and helping the patient to achieve a sense of self-esteem and self-affirmation, and a sense of safety in the transference with a corrective self-object. The process is still underway.

8. In its defensive role, splitting and projective identification are used by the infant to establish the state of invisibility of the self. Symptoms are painful reminders of those lost aspects of ourselves which are still entrapped in the nether world and which return to beckon our attention in grotesque pantomime

so as to remind us that we are not yet whole without them. They are the selves and objects of nameless dread who are awaiting the return of their names via our *re*-cognition of them. Our repentence in the depressive position is the ransom they demand. Yet, in the final analysis we must allow for the experience of Fate: Are we not, from another point of view, the projective materializations of our inscrutable scenarios helplessly *observing and betraying* ourselves via splitting and projective identification in the act of survival?

9. The patient utilizes normal projective identification in the form of externalization in his cooperation with the analyst, and defensive projective identification in his resistance to the analysis. The analyst's projective counteridentification is his own capacity to intercept projections; his capacity to give interpretations is due to his vicarious introspection, his empathy, and his imagination—all of which are the instruments of projective identification and splitting. His capacity to sort out the material in the patient's associations has to do with selection and recombination, a process which I call metathesis.

Kohut tells us that the infant normally forms a self-object representation which has bipolar configuration: one is a merger relationship with an idealized object and the other is a mirroring relationship by the self-object of a grandiose self. I believe that the idealized self-object representation is a way of talking about a projective identification by the self into an object which is needed to be idealized; therefore, the self-object has been created by the idealizing imagination of the self. On the other hand, the grandiose self is not only mirrored by a self-object, as Kohut suggests, but also is the result of a merger transference that is a result of a state of projective identification, as Rosenfeld and Kernberg have suggested. Thus, the grandiose self is a way of talking about an ad hoc identification with an idealized self-object representation through projective identification. Of particular significance to technique is the issue of how the analyst considers omnipotence in general and grandiosity and idealization in particular.

10. It is my impression of borderline and psychotic patients that they have from the very beginning suffered from insufficient and ill-directed omnipotence. To me, omnipotence is a mental blanket given us both by heriditary endowment *and* by the parental environment to help us deal with psychic strain by allowing us to postpone or suspend the awareness, meaning, impact, and significance of events. Thus, omnipotence is a prime requirement for pychotic, borderline, and narcissistic patients to restore or protect an enfeebled, embattled, and fragmented self. At the same time, they must have access to objects who themselves can be background objects of great stature, importance, and immutability so as to guarantee the prime scaffolding of their psychic space. The requirement for omnipotence probably has been underestimated by Kleinian writers—even though Klein herself (1935) did speak about the manic position alongside the depressive position and the paranoid-schizoid position, and, in so doing, seemed to indicate that she thought it was normal. Kohut and his predecessors, on the other hand, seem to ignore the boundary difficulties with omnipotence generally, and with destructive object transformations implicit in merger phantasies.

The dual-track system would make allowances for both points of view: the separate track of reality orientation on track one, and the continuation of primary identification with its omnipotent retinue on track two. The normal human being needs both tracks in an optimal interrelationship so as to achieve at-one-ment. The Background Object of Primary Identification is the vertex of the two tracks which emerge from it— very much like a double helix.

11. I do not believe that the psychoanalytic treatment of splits has achieved the importance that it deserves. When Freud secularized the splitting of the personality into impulses which were counterposed by repression, he unfortunately reduced splits to instinctual impulses and gave the impression that they were all connected somewhere in the id but separated only when they achieved consciousness directly or via their derivatives. I

believe that the clinical situation demonstrates the contrary. Drug and alcoholic addictions, for instance, show that the narcissistic aspect of the personality may certainly be under the control of a peremptory organization, but it has been my experience that this organization is, as a rule, split off and independent of the relatively normal adult person who brings the alcoholic (his split-off self) into treatment. More often than not, I have found that the split-off addictive aspect, for instance, has a motivation and a life-support system of its own. It seems to want alcohol, for instance, not necessarily because the patient himself is anxious, but rather because it believes it can get it due to a weakness in the personality.

The motivational system of a split-off self, in other words, is not so easily understood in terms of dynamic frustrations in the patient's life on a one-to-one basis. The motivations of split-off selves are far more complex; they seem to have a life of their own and act as parasites who are doing their best to preserve their own life agendas. The same can be said for melancholia, narcissistic disorders, and psychosis. The important aspect in the treatment of splits, therefore, is the recognition that they behave as if they were separate personages dwelling within the self-perimeter. Of utmost importance in understanding splitting clinically, however, is *premature closure,* that early form of extreme splitting which allows for dissociations in the personality to occur. In the psychoanalysis of these splits we must observe Bion's dictum to shift perspective and allow ourselves to "be the split" so as to see the psychic situation from that vertex.

Borderline dissociations represent split-off parts *(a)* within the self, or *(b)* in other people. When the splits are within the self, they may appear alternately or in a montage.

It must also be remembered that the various split-off subpersonalities which occupy the minds of neurotics, borderlines, and psychotics are not only split-off aspects of self, they are also intimately commingled with varying aspects of already internalized objects formed by projective identification and subsequent introjection, or by interpersonal objects which are projected into and then internalized. Some of these internalized objects may include superego objects and the ego-ideal. I hope to demonstrate some of these complications in the clinical examples.

12. Projective identification must be understood as a phenomenon which involves a subject and an object, whether the object is an intrapsychic one or an interpersonal one. The infant's first screams are a protest of narcissistic rage into the container-mother to let her know the experience the infant is having. We must hypothesize that the infant wishes its message will be heard so that mother can either change the experience by modifying reality or modify the intensity of the experience by being able to bear the infant's pain along with the infant. Thus the effective mother and the ideal mother receive the infant's complaints in order to effect corrective action, assist the infant in enduring pain, or postponing the solution of the event.

When the infant has reason to believe that its mother has been transformed by its projections, then the maternal object is experienced as having undergone a frightening transformation into a victim. Thereafter, this object becomes spoiled, unclean, profane, unholy, dangerous, and all subsequent projections into it are in the service of denial, negation, disavowal, and contempt. From another point of view it can be seen that the infant's protests to his mother are urgent "announcements" to her that it is about to fall prey to some internal predator. A mother's failure to hear this cry confirms upon her infant the suspicion that she has been spoiled or invaded by this fear and has become transformed by it and therefore is not only no longer a useful object but now a dangerous one. It is of utmost importance, in other words, to understand whether the infant's identifications convey a message to the object to transform the projections or whether the object has been transformed by them.

The sadistic aspect of the personality seeks a masochistic object in order to project its own unwanted victim self. Further, there is a projective identification of the libidinous aspect into the sadistic victim to justify that the "victim wants to be the victim." On the other hand, the victim "projects" into the sadist that he or she, the predator, "wants to pick on me." A further recompense for the masochist is that, by virtue of being the target of the sadist's projective identifications, he or she is then in line for a future entitlement and a moral justification for having been a martyr. The sadist, on the other hand, seeks the moralization of his perverse contempt and becomes the righteous protector of purity; thus, for example, the Nazis could justify the elimination of the Jews because they were not only the natural victims, but were also profane. The more the identity of the profane can be established, the more justified are all further sadistic projective identifications into the already profaned object(s).

The psychotic, on the other hand, may not have access to an object relationship whereby he or she can projectively identify, and therefore may *(a)* split off a twin aspect and project into that one, or *(b)* identify with the bad aspects of the self and project the good aspects into another object at a distance. The failure of either or both of these mechanisms eventuates in negative hallucination of the self, disavowal of reality, and an ego fragmentation.

So far I have been dealing with the spectrum of the projective transformations (projective transfigurations of the object) relative to the death instinct. The spectrum of the libidinal instinct and the epistemophilic instinct reveals parallel transformations. If the infant is able to engage its mother lovingly, then a superbly adaptive love bond forms. On the other hand, if the infant utilizes the already existing love bond in order to coerce its mother in order to evade its own agenda of maturation development, then libido has been misused, and a corrupted (seduced, traduced, manipulated) object emerges from the transformation—actually a victim and a future persecutor. The mother who is able to attend to her infant's authentic needs, who is able to resist coercion, seduction, and manipulation, emerges as a real, admirable transforming (not transformed) object. The infant and child whose aims are not stopped at the proper boundary runs the risk of developing a concept of a contemptible, all-too-well-known, predictable object. The mother's capacity to delineate the border of curiosity in proper doses and stages eventuates in an object who is mysterious and yet real. The infant and child can then have respect and awe for the unknowability of a real person.

THE DETECTION OF SPLITTING AND PROJECTIVE IDENTIFICATION IN THE CLINICAL SITUATION

Splitting is sometimes easy to observe in the clinical situation and at other times is more subtle. I have already referred to split transferences in which objects in the patient's daily life seem to be invested with feelings which are split off from the analyst or from himself or represent a dichotomy within them. For instance, if the analyst is held in a highly idealized position, then the negative transference may be split off and projected into objects on the outside. Patients who use splitting often complain that they are split off from their feelings or split off from their objects. The therapist can observe that patients who are split within themselves seem to be at war with themselves. They do not seem to be significantly in contact with their inner worlds or with the meaningfulness of their outer worlds. They may lead shallow existences and seem constantly fatigued by trying to keep the splits apart. Borderline, phobic, hysterical, and obsessive-compulsive patients typify this portrait. Often one sees glaring inconsistencies within a patient's personality make-up, and analytic investigation generally reveals deep splits within these personalities. Splits are frequently seen in married couples, in groups, and in institutions where one aspect of a person's personality may be unconsciously experienced as split off and relocated (projected) in the other mate or someone else in the institutional setting. All group formations, as Freud (1921) and Bion (1959b) have pointed out, involve the projection of the ego ideal from members of the group onto the group leader—in the form of authority and responsibility. The group members may also project their egos, ids, and superegos altogether onto the group leader, as with Jim Jones in Jonestown. Wynne and Singer (1963a,b) and Stierlin (1969) have called attention to the delegation of a particular member of the family as the one chosen to be ill by the other members of the family. Wynne and Singer have also found different kinds of splitting used in family conversations in affected families. One type of splitting is amorphously fragmentary and the other is extreme polarization. The delegated patient seems to be identified with either of these modes to an extreme.

Projective identification can be observed in a variety of ways. Some patients talk about how they have been "sleepwalking" throughout their lives. I have already discussed the patient who went into "lateral time." These patients describe states of confusion with objects alongside states of disorientation, trancelike states, and being very dependent on others for their thinking. These patients often experience being controlled by other objects or even seek control by objects because they seem not to be strong-minded. Patients who seem to idealize others constitute a special type of projective identification in which they seem to give over their own valuable feelings to the object at their own expense. On the other hand, one may find patients with depressive or borderline illness who seem to identify with their split-off helpless self and seem to assign their healthy self to idealized objects for "safekeeping." Patients with boundary problems, whether in terms of time or in terms of space, characterize projective identificatory confusion and disorientation. I was able to measure the progress of one borderline patient, a victim of extreme projective identification, by the way she parked her car in front of my building. When she first began the analysis, her car invaribly crossed the white markers. Gradually, as her tendency towards confusion with her objects was analyzed, the car became more properly parked. Amnesias for names and places, fear of crowds, and claustrophobia constitute telltale signs of projective identification.

All forms of manipulation, persuasion, ingratiation, or seduction involve projective identification in the sense that the subject wishes to control an object via influence and subterfuge which, at bottom, involve phantasies of entering into the body of the object in order to effect this control. Most commonly, we see projective identification in the clothes we wear, the cars we drive, the homes we live in, and all the trappings of our life that provide colorful semblance of protection, or such other purposes which in our remote ancestry were used as display behavior to ward off predators.

CLINICAL ILLUSTRATIONS

(A) Projective Identification in a Neurotic

A twenty-eight-year-old single screenwriter of hysterical disposition began writing a screenplay which involved a male and female lead with whom he became intensely involved and dreamed about on several occasions. The heroine was very beautiful, exciting, well-educated, and mysterious. In his actual life, she contained aspects of his mother and grandmother, but there was also more than a trace of his own idealized split-off female self. Once he formed her character in his narrative, he felt like a Pygmalion who had created a Galatea with whom he then fell in love.

The hero, on the other hand, was a less spectacular person, loaded with neurotic problems, and seemed to be the butt of fate who nevertheless managed to blunder his way through life successfully. The patient became quite excited when he contemplated his Galatea and sought her image in the external world—in vain. The fruitlessness of his search catapulted him into depressive episodes from which he would emerge with some difficulty. On the other hand, he found himself highly identified with the protagonist of the story and became, rather than dramatically depressed, wanly apathetic for long periods of time. Subsequently, he became quite critical of members of his parental family and was able to "re-assign" (reprojective identification) this unfortunate image into his whole family, including mother, father, sister, and two brothers. Behind the reassignment of this pathetic image to his family lay yet another problem. The patient was the eldest of four children. He had been particularly thrown when his next sibling, a brother, was born. He tormented this brother on many occasions. In subsequent years, when this brother's fortunes fared poorly, especially after tragically losing his wife in an accident, the patient became unusually depressed, aware of continuing guilt from childhood towards his brother. He then projectively assigned his own feelings of guilt to his family as a mass generalization (a physical "class action"). In other words, it was the defective family which caused everything to go awry, not the patient's brutal actions towards his brother. The patient was finally able to accept his fear of awareness of his own complicity in ruining his brother's life, following which ensued the long analytic attempt at granting himself amnesty.

As to the projective assignments of the characters in his novel, it gradually became apparent in the transference that he believed that I was doing to him what he was doing to his own characters; that is, I was creating a "nebbish" out of him and either represented the idealized Galetea whom he could not possess or kept a Galetea for myself. The "spell" seemed to subside with interpretations to that effect.

(B) Perverse Projective Identification
in a Neurotic Patient

Typical projective identification may take the form of an "exchange transfusion." A once dour, neurotically schizoid female patient entered the consultation room one Monday and asked how long I had had a large plant on top of my Chinese chest. While taking off her coat, she commented that she used to despair about her gardening abilities and had had difficulties in growing plants in her backyard but that lately she seemed to have become very lucky in that regard and had found her "green thumb." She then lay down on the couch and stated, "By the way, I don't like your plant!" Her subsequent associations referred to her continuing progress in her marital and professional life, but she was not sure whether she was making any progress in the analysis.

I made the following interpretation: "The weekend break caused you to feel that I had taken the good green breast with me for the weekend, leaving you with a barren and desolate backyard to cultivate. You then had a phantasy about entering into me, stealing my vendure, possessing it for yourself, and identifying with it as the possessor of a 'green thumb' which had no connection with me, and therefore you owed me no gratitude. At the same time, I am now believed to be the container of your undesired barren self which cannot make things grow. We have exchanged roles."

The patient responded by stating that it was true that she had made progress in amny areas of her life but did not know whether this progress was due to the analysis or to other factors. It was also true that she had experienced a very barren weekend, yet she was not thinking of me or the analysis. She did not know what to think of me since I did not very often come to mind. Then she seemingly broke the thread of associations and began to deprecate other analysts in the community. I was able to suggest that the deprecated analysts were displacements of a me into whom she had cast her bad parts, and that her well-being could be thought of as those aspects of me which she had taken over for herself in her own work but was unwilling to associate benefit-wise with the analysis for fear that I might steal it back. Her only response was that she understood my interpretation but did not know whether she agreed, yet it was ture that lately she felt uneasy about feeling better.

The analysis later revealed that, when she unconsciously experienced herself as robbing me of my creativity and assigning it to herself, she was reinforcing an omnipotent image of herself fused with a female ego-ideal (anima) on one hand and a male ego-ideal (animus) on the other.

(C) Projective Identification in
a Narcissistic Character

The patient, a young married physician, began to realize in the course of the analysis that he acquired information by presuming he already possessed it, and that realizing the knowledge was simply a reminder rather than a learning for the first time. An associated omnipotent belief was that everything he learned—and everyone whose name he learned—became appended to him as slaves or satellites, so that he believed himself to be able to have knowledge about them and to be able to predict their future. This applied to all his friends, colleagues, and acquaintances. This alleged capacity for prediction amounted less to prophecy than to the need for the absence of surprise when developments in their lives took place. The analysis was able to untangle the intense omnipotent and omniscient investment in the projective identificatory notion that the patient had, in effect, created these objects and was only rediscovering them.

(D) Projective Identification in Exhibitionism and Voyeurism

I wish briefly to report on a case of exhibitionism and voyeurism in a young single man of twenty-three. The only child of a well-to-do divorced couple, he was referred to me by an attorney, having been apprehended by the police in the act of exhibiting himself from his apartment. The patient was psychologically-minded and cooperated with the analysis quite well. After considerable analysis, punctuated by more than an occasional relapse, the patient was able to see that he basically experienced himself as a very frightened, ungrown-up person who had developed a sophisticated false self of pseudo-maturity but was frightened of and ill-prepared for his emotional life. As a consequence, he tried to commandeer the images of women voyeuristically by pretending that his eyes (long-distance receptors) were hands and arms which could grasp and possess them. When he exhibited his penis, it, too, was believed to be a powerful organ which would capture the woman's attention and seduce her into being his sexual slave. The eyes were as secretive and stealthy as the penis was public for his omnipotent purposes. Each was felt to have power to enter into the body of the woman and take possession of her. Yet, behind his need to do this seemed to be lack of confidence in his background support—that is, in the Background Self-Object of Primary Identification, both mother and father.

(E) Projective Identification as
Restortation in a Case of Depression

The following is a case I have seen in psychotherapy on a once-weekly basis from time to time over the years. Although my attitude has been invariably analytic, I nevertheless have had the countertransference feeling that I was doing continuous "cardiopulmonary resuscitation" with a beleaguered, drowning young man. He was the eldest son of an heiress, Christian mother and a Jewish father, and had three younger siblings. There was an older sibling who died by drowning about a year before he was born. Upon his birth, his mother was so distraught with depression from the loss of her first child that he was sent to a foster home to be raised by foster parents. He was summoned by his parents to come home to live with them when he was about three or four. His father was chronically depressed and, upon learning of his wife's having an open affair, committed suicide when the patient was eleven. The patient never stopped grieving over the loss of his father. In the transference I quickly became his other father and have remained so ever since.

Recently, after a long hiatus, he came back to see me. Now an attorney, like his father, he is employed by a prominent industry in the legal office. He is married and has two children, yet has very little happiness in his life. Moreover, he recently began to suffer from hyperventilation and extreme anxiety attacks. The more successful he is in his own life, the more discrepancy there is with the success of his father. The patient also feels guilty for having lived one year longer than his father. During this particular hour he reported a dream in which his father was trying to talk to him as if he were under water, and his words were muffled. The patient's younger brother was also in the dream and was stubborn, petulant, and interfering, as if he did not want to let the father talk. The patient's associations were to his own hyperventilation and to his feelings of numbness. He stated poignantly, "My body is angry with me, and it won't let me in!"

I was able to interpret to the patient that he was identified (projectively) with the link-attacking younger brother on one hand, but he was also suffocatingly identified with a dead father under water—as well as with a drowned, dead older brother whose fate cast a tragic spell across the whole family's fortunes. Somehow this interpretation had a dramatic effect on the patient. His demeanor lightened as never before. He then had a visual image of his father sitting on the couch in the family home, and recalled sitting there with him the last time they had a conversation together before his father committed suicide. I suggested to the patient that he seemed to have allowed his father to come to life from under the water—an internal father who seems to be wanting to contact and speak with him. What followed was very moving: the patient began to talk to his father in my office as if I were not even there. The conversation included aspects of the original conversation that was held twenty-one years ago, and then the patient brought his father up to date about his progress. He told his father that he was married, had two children, and was now a lawyer just like him. The father seemed very happy and proud and asked the patient to visit him again.

The dream, and the interpretation of it, in some mysterious way, apparently freed the patient from a state of life-long projective identification with his dead brother (and dead father) and allowed him to projectively recreate a father before the tragedy. He could have a relationship with his restored father to whom he could give life and with whom he could have companionship.

(F) Projective Identification in the
Service of Defense of the Superego

Although it is generally true that projective identification is used by infants (and patients) in the service of evading reality, it is also their way of pinpointing reality—that is, a reality that may confirm one's preconceptions. Side by side with projection into reality is the special need of an infant to defend the goodness of that defective parental environment at his own expense, a phenomenon which Fairbairn (1941, 1943, 1944, 1946, 1949) has called the *defense of the superego*. By this term, Fairbairn means that the infant is dependent upon his parents for his life support and has no alternatives or options. As a result, the infant has to defend the rightness of the cosmos in which he is living by absolving the parental environment of all blame and accepting the blame himself. It is the obverse of what Klein has called the paranoid-schizoid position, in which the infant projects its bad feelings onto the parental object. Precociously mature, depressed infants and children may be able to detect their parents' need to project into them as a means of "curing" themselves of their bad feelings. Thus, children may be the all-too-knowing receptacles of parental projections as well as the originators of them. Some of these children think that survival depends upon being the recepticle of projections and they steel themselves in a depressive, masochistic defense armor to withstand the onslaught with the belief that they are "curing" the parent and then awaiting their turn to be loved. Thus, the parents are "purified," and the children become the "sacrificial Christ," so to speak, as a genuine gift of reparation for a crime they own up to, knowing they never committed it.

The dual-track system that I have often referred to in this volume unites both theories. The infant who knows about the dreadful reality it confronts must make allowances for its objects and maintain that its parents are good and that the world is good and is administered by a god that is good—so there is hope for a sinner who can repent and be pure again. On another track this selfsame infant is aware of being persecuted by an external environment which may be hostile, defective, or impinging, and which may, as a result, evoke its destructive impulses which are then projected into this reality on the phantasy track. The following case vignette demonstrates some of these issues.

A thirty-five-year-old screenwriter, depressed to one degree or another throughout most of his life, came into analysis after having been left by his wife, whom he loved dearly and continues to pine for. The marriage had lasted twelve years during which his wife's severe depressive episodes led to a long hospitalization, after which there was a deteriorative personality change, according to the patient. As his professional fortunes improved, hers deteriorated, and she finally left him. From time to time, she would contact him briefly, without actually having any intimate relationship with him.

Almost as soon as the patient was born his father, a physician, had left for overseas duty in World War II. The patient heard about his father from his mother and saw his picture but couldn't believe in his reality. He longed for him to return and felt grateful when he finally did. The patient described a very impoverished relationship with his mother who apparently had an affair while his father was overseas, causing the patient to feel impotent and shameful because he couldn't preserve Mother for Father. When Father returned, he was very much involved with setting up his own practice and seemed to ignore his son. Years of analysis brought reluctant revelations that the patient believed his father to be a selfish, narcissistic person who was interested only in himself and not in his family. The patient, on the other hand, doted on his father and did everything to please him, and submitted obsequiously to his father's usually unwarranted criticism.

In the course of the analysis the patient's transference was displaced onto his ex-wife. It gradually became apparent that his ex-wife, for whom he continued to pine, was a borderline psychotic who often went into delusional episodes in which she would be very critical of him—his religion, his parents, his analyst—whereas he would go far out of his way to see to her welfare, give her money, bring her food, make sure she went to doctors, etc. From a clinical standpoint, one could say this patient was masochistic. More to the point, however, was that his wife, like his father previously, was his private addictive religion. As long as she was all right, he felt happy. He believed he could "wait out" her indifference because "she would change." He could tolerate more suffering than she could give punishment. "Maybe it'll someday be my turn to get good treatment from her," he would say sorrowfully.

It finally became apparent that he idealized her not only as a displacement from his image of his narcissistic father, but she was also a projective identification of his own pathetic, infantile, helpless self which he could only nourish and attend to at a distance. Insofar as she was a parent imago, however, she had to be preserved because, like "Tinkerbell," he observed, "If I stop believing in her, she'll die!" She represented, in other words, the projective identification of hope which he dared not contain within himself. She was the carrier of his good self, and he was the carrier of her bad self. Like the troubadors of yore, he was willing to suffer a life without hope as long as he was living in a world where she was a goddess. The patient stated, "If I stop being unhappy, then there is danger that everybody will die and the world will disappear!" At this time, the patient followed this remark with, "But, damn it! I want my turn now!"

This case represents an extreme example of a patient who could absorb the badness of his parents and identify with it himself (introjectively) and project his own good qualities into them in order to live in a world where hope was possible and where God was alive and perfect. The object he is trying to restore is the Background Object of Primary Identification (the background self-object), which is to become the superego or, as I prefer to call it, the Object of Destiny—insofar as it is believed to be the object which has his future in its safekeeping and guides him to his future.

(G) Projective Identification in a
Neurotic Patient: A Brief Vignette

A twenty-nine-year-old teacher came to me for analysis stating that she had problems with sex and also felt very anxious and immature. When I asked her why she sought me out to be her analyst, she stated that she had heard me give a lecture and knew that she needed to get something *back* from me. I was flattered by her statement but was curious about the use of the word "back." The patient was also curious. It finally emerged that she believed that I was strangely familiar to her insofar as I reminded her of her own past. Ultimately, the analysis revealed that I really reminded her of an aspect of herself, a longed-for male aspect (an animus), which would have strength and would be able to lead her, much like an internal big brother. I believe this is another example of the original conception of projective identification as elucidated by Freud (1914b) in "Narcissism: An Introduction" when he talked about the splitting-off and projection of the ego-ideal.

(H) Projective Identification in a
Case of Drug Addiction

Patients who are afflicted with drug abuse display splitting and projective identification in several different ways. I should like to refer briefly to a patient who had been addicted to codeine for nearly twenty years, and whose habit happily succumbed to analytic treatment. At the time he entered analysis, he was a forty-one-year-old practicing physician suffering from lifelong depression and schizoid withdrawal. Although married and the father of two children, it was difficult for him to be sanguine about his married life, although he had enjoyed playing with his son when the latter was young. The patient suffered from severe migraine headaches which instigated the codeine addiction.

Early in the analysis he reported a childhood memory in which he had awakened from a nap and, looking across the room at the entrance into the hallway, he saw scary phantoms which terrified him. Later he discovered that these phantoms were really the clothes that were hanging on an indoor clothesline in his midwest home. The associations were such that I was enabled to interpret the destructive aspects of his own feces which had been projected onto the clothesline and were felt to have become persecutory demons. Behind his fear of the omnipotent destructiveness of his own feces was his belief that his mother had already become a victim of his feces, was too depressed, and therefore too much a victim to be able to be useful to him. She could only be frightening because she was a victim and therefore had to be avoided. The same was true for his father who also appeared depressed and victimized. In short, the patient believed that there was no one who could stand him or take care of him, so he withdrew into a quasi-autistic shell.

In retrospect, I believe one would call this patient alexithymic insofar as he had been so frightened of his feelings that he disowned them. His organismic panic was never experienced as being transformed into signal anxiety by maternal and paternal self-objects, that is, anticipatory anxiety appropriate to the stimulus. His organismic panic was unabated when he entered the analysis, and codeine seemed to be the only cure.

As the analysis continued, it became clearer that he had given over his ego, superego, and id to another aspect of himself, a split-off self, a twin, which then took omnipotent control. He also managed to relate to objects in the external world who would take care of him and protect him from confrontations with life. This mysterious twin became more and more ruthless, peremptory, and influencing. Sometimes the patient dreamed of this organization as a mafia composed of many powerful, corrupt, and dangerous people. He was now in their power, they were diabolical, and he could not get out. They were "in the drug traffic" and demanded that he be their agent to get them drugs, and he, having sold his soul to them, was unable to say no. Meticulous examination of the nature of this corrupt and demoniacal suborganization yielded dividends, and the patient was able to give up his habit and to ease his depression and his experience of migraine.

This patient represents another example of a dissociated split within the self—a twin—which became the focus for multiple projective identifications of aspects of one self into another self. In pictorial imagery, the case represents a perverse example of the siamese twin in which the infant is sitting on the lap of the Background Object. Thus, this self-object picture is one in which the object behind the self is malevolent, corrupt, and controlling, and the child sitting on its lap is its hapless victim.

(I) Projective Identification in a
Schizoid Borderline Patient

A sad, beautiful, youthfully fortyish, single female attorney came into analysis because of lifelong feelings of emptiness and deadness. She was born and raised in another country during time of war and had experienced a great deal of horror and uprooting. She experienced her mother as being terrified, immature, and unable to be a mother. Her father was a more effective parent when the patient was young, but later she learned that he suffered from psychotic illness; he had to be hospitalized every year, and died of a stroke when she was still in her teens.

In a dream early in the analysis she imagined herself to be a piece of lucite. Multiple associations led to feelings of being frozen or of plastic deadness, by which she was telling me that she believed herself to be stuck in a frozen, plastic, lucite state, and that she was still in the state of shock which she had entered in her infancy. One day she had a dream about being at a movie theater and fearing that she would be unable to get to the movie because the line was too long. She had to urinate and was unable to find a public restroom outside the theater. Someone told her to go inside the theater, which she did, but there seemed to be a lot of children in front of her. The patient's association to the movie house was: "I didn't know I had to use the 'movie house' to explain my feelings. I didn't know that I didn't know my feelings. I am dead, frozen. My hopeful self is out there in my loved ones."

This dream represented many different levels and aspects of projective identification. First of all, it represented her fear that she would not be able to continue the analysis (for external reasons) and would be unable, therefore, to project her feelings. As Bion (1959a) pointed out, psychotic and borderline patients, rather than suffering from projections, suffer from the inability to project insofar as they lack the objects that can contain the projections. She was thus experiencing me as an obstructive object who could not and would not contain her projections. I was finally able to see, from other material dispersed across the whole analysis, that she experienced me to be a mother and father who would not and could not take her in—that is, allow myself to be pregnant with her. She wanted me to allow her back in the womb so as to give her that prenatal comfort which she needed before she could lead her life. Her fear was that I could not tolerate her regression. She reported a dream in which she was wrapped tightly in a warm blanket lying on my couch, and I, sitting behind her, was bare chested. Her associations were that she was wrapped tightly up against my body where my skin was the blanket.

This patient taught me someting of crucial and general importance about projective identification. One of the principle motives of projective identification, particularly "normal autistic" projective identification, is the infant's desire to go back into the hibernative protection of the womb *with mother's permission.* Patients who wish to go back into the womb, and who do not have mother's permission, cannot enter into this protective state of projective identification and therefore become clincally autistic and later psychotic or borderline. Drugs, perversions, fragmentations, and many pathological states constitute forlorn attempts to achieve a makeshift projective identification, that is, a sanctuary in lieu of being permitted to be back into the grace of mother's womb with the promise of love, safety, and self-affirmation.

Thus, this patient epitomizes two principle aspects of projective identification: *(a)* the desire to have mother's permission to reenter the state of blessed womblike, hibernative sanctuary (primary at-one-ment with the Background Object of Primary Identification); and *(b)* the projective identification of one's stressful feelings into an interpersonal self-object who is capable of being a worthy, transforming container for these feelings, one who can permit the expression of these feelings and give them meaning.

(J) Projective Identification in a Patient with Zonal Confusion: A Brief Vignette

A young secretary was twenty-four when she entered analysis with me, single, and complained of difficulties in getting close to men. No sooner had the analysis started than weekend breaks and vacations mobilized an excited, erotic transference to me. Sexual feelings began to emerge in superabundance. I was gradually able to show the patient that the frustration created by the breaks and vacations were causing her to experience a flood of excitement from her mouth and tongue to her vagina, and this excitement had transformed her image of the breast nipple into the future daddy's penis. By this, I meant that frustration had caused her to abandon her oral interest in feeding since the breast had abandoned her and, instead, to "rush into her future" to get to the future penis—in other words, to precipitate the arrival of a precocious oedipus complex.

The patient associated to her distress at my going away. I told the patient that her mouth, her rectum, and her genitals were all getting together to complain about my leaving, on one hand, and were also celebrating my going away by having a ruckus, evacuative, genital party to celebrate their freedom from Mommy's restraint and authority. The patient seemed to be relieved by the interpretation. I was calling attention to the commingling of the zones.

(K) Projective Identification in the
Case of a Chronic Schizophrenic

The patient is a twenty-nine-year-old single white male who had a psychotic break during his early adolescence, had been seen by many psychiatrists, and had been often hospitalized. At the time of my seeing him, he had already presumably become a chronic schizophrenic. Our working alliance developed slowly and tentatively at the beginning of the treatment. Although living at home because he had no permanent job and no means of supporting himself, his feelings towards his mother and father were unabashedly hostile. It was not too long before his hateful feelings towards them became expressed in the transference towards me. Like them, I was felt to be a very controlling, suffocating person who would not allow him to have a life of his own.

During the course of one analytic hour, he began to take a cigarette out of a cigarette pack, then thought better of it, and put it back. When I inquired into the gesture, he said that he had changed his mind about wanting to smoke. When I pushed my inquiry, he said that he did not want to smoke because, if he did smoke, he would cause me to become a cigarette smoker.

Had this man been a neurotic patient, I would have understood that his hesitancy in smoking might have had to do with care about manners, deportment, my rules, etc., and that perhaps his fear might have been that I might be discomfited by his smoking. I have heard from a great number of patients their fear that their tobacco smoke might "poison" me. With this particular patient, however, the matter was quite different. He was afraid that his smoking would not only "poison" me but it would convert me—influence me—into becoming his own smoking self, which he despised. He was therefore in contact with his primary process (alpha function) to such a degree that it apparently was unmodified; his smoking would convert me into a cigarette smoker. By this I understood him to mean that his action had magically omnipotent power, the kind one sees in the archaic "thinking" of catatonic schizophrenics, in which their wishes or actions have immediate and powerful influences upon the rest of the world because they are the center of that world.

Behind this belief was a long history I was able to gather of a patient who had mentally "disappeared" over the years and had, in effect, gotten rid of his feelings *and* the mind which could have feelings about his vulnerable, sensitive, and enormously fragile state of mind. Thus, he lacked that filtering, reasoning capacity, even when projecting, to know that at worst he might have been influencing me through his vapors but not transforming me altogether. The totality of the exchange between us is pathognomonic for schizophrenic psychosis because of the very immediacy, directness, and totality of the "switch." It is as if his wish became God's command even though he may not have been sure that he wished it.

Even though my interpretations seemed to relieve the patient of his fear that he could turn me into a cigarette smoker, there was nevertheless another self, a mad one, which would experience even more humiliation because of the obvious impotence of his wishes. I chose to talk of his sense of shame and humiliation about his failure to turn me into a cigarette smoker—and that yielded greater results, I believe, than if I had dealt with his fear of the power of his omnipotent designs. My choice was in line with my belief that psychotic patients, although they may think and demonstrate their belief in omnipotence and omniscience, are, at bottom, merely trying to "practive" or "rehearse" those techniques of omnipotence that they "never quite got right" the first time around, and they therefore more fear the failure of the enactment of their wishes than their actualization. When I was able to understand this profound sense of narcissistically humiliating weakness, the patient began to respond, and his delusions of reference and of influence began to subside. I also ultimately was to learn that his desire for me not to be transformed into a cigarette smoker had to do with his need for me to be kept ideal or sacred and in no way contaminated by any aspect of his own profane self.

(L) Prototypical Projective Identification in a Neurotic Patient: A Brief Vignette

This thirty-three-year-old married university professor entered analysis because of many inhibitions, one of which was sexual. During the course of the analysis he began to explore the origin of his feelings about sex and, concurrently, began to get excited about a highly seductive young secretary in his office. Sensing his vulnerability and receptivity (he claimed), she began seriously to seduce him, and he found himself tempted and afraid. He and I were able to see that this seductive woman represented, among many other things, a projective identification of his own peremptory urges—all the erupting neediness—which were attempting to surface into awareness. These urges always intimidated him as if they were someone else impinging into him. On the other hand, he experienced me, the analyst, as the one who *evokes* these feelings within him currently (as mother or father did long ago), which seems to necessitate his projection of these feelings into someone else. Thus, I too was a bearer of his projective identifications—in this case, of a stimulating object who had become an exciting object (the excitement of feelings).

Finally, the patient was able to unite the two projective identifications—as a sexual mother trying to have sex with me and a me having sex with her (by my projecting exciting, evocative feelings into him), so that he became a locale where a primal scene was taking place. Thus, his inhibition was a magical control of the parental intercourse. As long as he was projectively-introjectively identified with a sexual mother and a sexual father, he *(a)* could omnipotently keep them separated inside, and *(b)* could via his own inhibitions keep them from having intercourse, and he felt reassured—at a price. At the same time, he felt himself to be the hapless, "unconsulted" interface or medium for two objects to transact through.

This typical deployment of projective identification (and splitting) demonstrates the use of one's own body self as an effigy—in the image of the siamese-twin of one head controlling two bodies. It ultimately was revealed that he had, additionally, projectively assigned his prey-predator fears to his parents so that their having sex was frightening, insofar as it represented a later (sexualized) version of a more primitive fear of one parent eating or victimizing the other. He had not yet learned that, when bodies get together, they pleasurably explore each other as alternative to destroying one another.

(M) Projective Identification in a Borderline Patient: Breakthrough of a Chronic, Characterological Impasse

The patient is a thirty-three-year-old actor who has been in analysis with me for one year following what he claims was an unsuccessful analysis elsewhere. His first analyst simply could not "break through my defenses." During the next to the last visit prior to my summer vacation, the patient reported a dream. He was lying in bed, and a prostitute was sticking her tongue onto his penis through the urethra and up into the bladder. It was disgusting. She seemed to turn into a witch. His associations to the dream were that when he awakened the following morning, he had a sick stomach feeling, felt nauseous, and felt he might like to vomit. He also found himself groaning. The groaning and the feeling somehow reminded him of a woman during intercourse. His next associations were to the sound of his mother's groaning during intercourse which he had overhead as a child.

I interpreted to him that his bladder was full of feelings from his stomach about a mommy-me who was going away for a holiday with her analytic husband and taking the breast from him. His anger toward this thought is expressed as a urinary attack against the breast which then turns it into a bad groaning feeling in his stomach. He wishes to get rid of this by urinating into a mommy who can take away this pain and clean up the mess within him. Yet his anger is justified from his point of view because my pleasure with my mother is felt to endanger him by taking my care from him and giving it elsewhere.

The patient said, "You're way off today, Grotstein!"

I then interpreted to the patient that, indeed, my interpretation may have been "way off" or might have been "right on." His fear of accepting the interpretation has to do, I suggested, with a fear that his urine had turned a caretaking "toilet breast" mommy-me—who was trying to help him with his pain by taking it away—into a victim of his urinary attack and into a person who would then, as a witch, urinate right back into him.

The patient became quite startled and said, "My god, you're right!" He went on to recall that he was frightened to have a close relationship with anybody with empathic concern for him because of a fear that his own neediness is bad, and that the person becomes transformed by it into somebody who is either damaged or damaging. He has to cut off the communication the moment he believes someone is of any help to him. As soon as he said, "I have to cut them off immediately!" he had a visual image of my cutting off his genitals with a knife. He then offered the opinion that his own neediness was the cause of his wife's cancer. I was able to talk to the patient about his experience of a long history of empathic failures in which he had gotten the idea that his own neediness, including his urinary needs, was bad and destructive (there was considerable background material of his belief that this was so). He then said that he was frightened when he saw me as empathic because then he could destroy me. I then opined that he felt much safer in being allied with the denying people in his life than being the needy one who has to suffer being denied. He said, "My stomach pain seems to be gone, and it's no longer smoggy outside."

Of key importance in this case, which resembles so many others in analysis, especially borderline and psychotic patients, is that severe resistances and negative therapeutic reactions tend to take place because of the very effectiveness of the therapist in being able to understand the patient's projective identifications as communications of urgent needs. When the analyst becomes confused with the projections *(a)* as victim and *(b)* as victimizer, the patient receives a double dose of terror: first, in being vulnerable to persecutory anxiety and guilt for having created a damaged object; and, second, because of creating a hostile, destructive therapist who then reprojects (urinates or defecates) on him. Understandably, therefore, the patient must then cut off communication before his feelings return via a boomerang trajectory.

(N) Projective Identification in an
Obsessive-Compulsive Neurotic

The patient is a thirty-eight-year-old married engineer. Noteworthy in his past history was his having felt close to his mother and grandmother and distant from his father, whom he felt very afraid of when he was younger and contemptuous later. A series of dreams about bowel movements allowed the patient to associate to conscious preoccupations with his anus and to memories of anal masturbation when he was a child. The dreams about the bowel movements were associated with sadistic attacks against father figures in his current life. Finally, it emerged that he identified his feces with his father and the more he had been afraid of his father, the more he would clamp down on the feces with his rectal musculature. Thus, the first projective identification was one in which he projected a father image into the feces and then proceeded to control it through the manic defenses of triumph, contempt, and control.

However, he found that this sometimes led to fear of having a bowel movement because no sooner did he have the triumphant relief that he had anally destroyed his father and flushed him down the toilet than another father came to fill up his rectum. Thus, the process repeated itself, and he learned in the analysis that he had become a prisoner to his own manic defense of sadistic triumph over his father. More to the point was the phantasy that the image of the father which was reflected in the feces was a combined image—of a hostile, fearsome father who frightened him, and of a disappointing, castrated, shameful father for whom he had contempt. The more he vented his sadistic impulses upon this father image in the feces, the more victimized the father became, and therefore the more terrifying each time he returned via the next bowel movement. The obsessive-compulsive defenses were attempts to keep the victimized, profane father at a distance.

Manic defenses, especially those utilized in obsessive-compulsive neurosis, such as reaction formation, doing-undoing, isolation, etc., combine splitting and projective identification in very interesting ways. The more the anal-sadistic manic mechanisms attack the enemy and turn this former predator into a victim (prey), the more dangerous the victim becomes because of the fear of being contaminated by the dangerous essence of the victim. If one touches a victim—a leper, for instance—then one catches that propensity. In my own clinical experience, predators seem to be, paradoxically, less frightening than are their victims. Thus, identification with the aggressor, which this patient certainly experienced, seems at first blush to be a safe measure to hide from danger, whereas identification with the victim of the predator is the most fearful thing one can imagine because of the absolute vulnerability associated with it. Thus, this patient's lifelong struggle was to keep his good side (identification with mother) split off from what he felt to be the bad side (identification with father) which he wished to disavow (disidentify from) and project his own bad self into father. The bad self he was projecting into father was *(a)* his own hostile feelings insofar as he was afraid of father attacking him (which never happened), and *(b)* his own sense of impotence, shameful-ness, and vulnerability which in turn was associated with feelings of dependency.

Sadism and masochism are ritualized attempts to repeat prey-predator anxiety with the hope of conquering it—either by being the predator (sadist) who keeps the projected prey in the victim, or by being the masochist, who, by being the victim, can become a better victim than the sadist can be predator—but to little avail in either case because each maneuver creates phantom persecuting victims anew. Thus, they are fated to remain forever in each other's embrace—at arm's distance.

PROJECTIVE IDENTIFICATION IN COUNTERTRANSFERENCE

Projective identification is intimately involved in the phe-nomenon of countertransference. Grinberg (1979) differentiates between projective counteridentification and coun-tertransference by associating the latter with the analyst's own neurosis which the patient's presence or associations evoke and which are idiosyncratic to the analyst, and identifying the former as those feelings which are specific for the patient who is projecting them into the analyst but which would probably be felt by any analyst seeing that patient. Projective counteriden-tification, in other words, corresponds to the analyst's signal of the presence of the patient's feelings inside his own self in an affective state of extraterritoriality. The whole issue of coun-tertransference in modern psychoanalysis has been recently reviewed by Epstein and Feiner (1979). The analytic psycho-therapist can detect countertransference and projective coun-teridentification by alteration in his state of mind while listening to a patient. The experiences range from sleepiness to anxiety, loneliness, aloneness, jealousy, envy, violence, deadness, rage, dread, depression, confusion, disorientation, need to be active, desire (sexual and other), boredom (starving), the feeling of being flooded—to mention but a few. The therapist's container capacity, like Bion's container prism, is hopefully able to transform these experiences into the waveband of the color spectrum of meaning.

I myself have been alert to many countertransferences or projective counteridentificatory feelings. Specifically, I am particularly sensitive when patients, as they frequently want to do, reach out to the white wall next to the couch in my office and spread their desperate hand against the flat surface. I invariably have the feeling that my body is being touched, caressed, or poked.

I should like to present a poignant example of a very special case of countertransference (projective counteridentification) which illustrates projective identification with a special clarity. The patient entered analysis with me because of fears associated with her adjustment to her husband and to living in the United States (she came from a central European country). Normally sprite and infectious, she suddenly interrupted an hour one day by getting up from the couch and going over to my consultation chair to sit silently for approximately twenty minutes. She appeared to be in a trance, and somehow I began to feel myself to be in a trance as well. I found myself to be speechless. It was as if a spell had overtaken both of us. Gradually, I began to feel terribly and unaccountably uncomfortable and then experienced the eerie feeling that I was dying. I continued to say nothing but began to feel even worse. Finally the patient broke the silence by saying, "I had the feeling I was dying just then and that you were dying too!" She became tearfully animated and told me the following story.

Her parents had divorced when she was three years of age. According to the custody laws in that country at the time, the father obtained child custody. He sent her to be raised by his parents in a remote village in the high Alps. She became very close to her grandparents, although she often would visit and be visited by her mother. When she was six or seven, her father sent for her to return to the city so that she could be educated. The separation of the parents from each other, and her from them, had already been a severe enough trauma, but having to separate from her beloved grandparents seemed to have crushed her. She remembered the morning at the train station when she said goodbye to them. She believed that she was dying and also that her grandparents were dying at that moment.

This analytic hour occurred on an anniversary of that tragic moment of loss. I had become confused by her with a dying her and a dying grandparental couple. I never again would minimize the power and accuracy, to say nothing of the poignancy, of projective counteridentification.

This case represents one of the principle aspects of projective identification which I wish to draw to the reader's attention, that of communication. There are certain feelings which are so constructed that they seem to be beyond words and may, therefore, have been before words when first experienced. Powerful feelings are more often than not expressed by giving another person the experience of how one feels. Throughout the course of human history, dialogue and confession seem to have been dominant forms of emotional release. All human beings seem to have the need to be shriven, that is, to be relieved of the burden of unknown, unknowable feelings by being able to express them, literally as well as figuratively into the flesh, so to speak, of the other so that this other person can know how one felt. The sadist and the murderer desire to see the look of agony on their victim's face so as to be sure that the murderer's own tortured experience can be transmitted through the network of projective identification to the victim whose agonized face completes the communication—"over and out!" How else can a beleaguered patient know that his analyst understands than if he suffers that experience which the patient lacks the words to describe? That is why I have come to the belief—and insist upon the definition—that all projection is projective identification, from the vantage point of the projector. We each are projectors and ultimately wish the other to know the experience we cannot communicate or unburden ourselves of until we have been convinced that the other understands. We cannot be convinced that they understand until we are convinced that they now contain the experience. Projection into a vacuum is not projection. It always has to have meaning, and meaning is the suffering of the flesh and the spirit of the other, whether the "other" is an internal object, an object representation, or a person.

Reflective Recapitulations

Normal splitting and projective identification are the beneficent legacies of a series of self-objects which can now be seen as the harmonious cooperation of intrapsychic and interpersonal objects. In infancy it takes three people to lead one life, the life of the infant; in adulthood, it takes two—at least. Thus, mother and father are linked together in siamese twinship with the infant who itself links up with this siamese bond with its own inherent Background Object of Primary Identification.

Abnormal splitting and projective identification emerge from infantile mental catastrophe, disappointment, dissolution, and despair. Thus, the therapist who wishes to acknowledge the importance of splitting and projective identification must allow himself to become "pregnant" with his patient's material not only so as to be able to be receptive to the patient's preverbal, primitive *communication,* but also to be able to allow the patient the achievement of *autistic relatedness* guaranteed by a Background Object of Primary Identification, the achievement of *symbiotic relatedness* guaranteed by the interpersonal self-object, and the reasonable guarantee of the *hope of a future* by the reestablishment of a relationship with the object of destiny.

Thus, the therapist who treats a patient enters into an epigenetically predetermined sequence of relationships which I have called "siamese bonding." These include autistic, symbiotic, and separated-individuated relatedness. By this I mean that the therapist engages in a dual-track relationship with the patient *and* in the understanding of the person's material insofar as the relationship is both real and in phantasy, and insofar as the patient is reporting his empathic failures in present and past realities which have both real and phantasy components. I am advising the therapist, in other words, to play two hands at the piano rather than one, so to speak. I hope I have demonstrated my reasons for this in the case histories of the psychotic patients. Although I believe it is very important to detail the patient's employment of defensive splitting and projective identification, I consider it even more important to help establish an autistic and symbiotic bonding with the patient so that the content of interpretations of splitting and projective identification can be seen as the "best possible solutions" that the patient could make under the circumstances (Pao 1979).

We see from the case histories that these patients invariably had to resort to the use of defensive splitting and projective identification because of their feelings of enfeeblement and helplessness. In their attempts to rescue themselves they have compounded their miseries by creating a double anxiety—the results of splitting and projective identification and the cost to ego cohesiveness that it betokens. The infant and the patient want their objects to be background objects which can be a backboard for the reflection of their thoughts and a transformative object who can "catch," sort out, and reflect upon the projections so as to give significance and meaning to the patient's productions. *From another point of view, it can be said that the existence of projective identification ultimately depends upon the receiver of it. The more empathic the therapist object is with the patient's projective identifications, the less projective and identifying they are and the more they become communications which can have self-transcendent meaning for the patient. At the same time, projective identifications for which the patient is not ready for reflection must be contained within the domain of postponement by the therapist so that the patient does not have to resort to psychotic disavowal or eradication of his or her state of mind.*

It must also be remembered that infants and patients are keenly susceptible to the projections of their parents and their therapist, as Langs has so beautifully pointed out. Thus, therapy is indeed a bipersonal field with the possibility of projective identifications and splitting going across the network in both directions. That is why we must be especially in touch with the patient's experience of us as therapists so as to be in tune with our own empathic failures which may have resulted in our own projective identifications into and onto the patient, which then reroute him from his own scenario onto ours.

Splitting and projective identification create the internal objects of the inner world as scaffoldings for the development of future psychic structures. The design of the creation follows the protocol of all the possible relationships between the parts of the infant's subjective self (mouth, anus, genital, skin, sense organs, mind, etc.) and the corresponding anatomy of the object's body. The linkages follow instinctual motivations or, as I prefer to call them, after Bion, L, H, and K functions, where L stands for love, nurture, slumber, etc.; H stands for hate, aggression, defense, preparation, repairing, and taking care of; and K stands for knowledge, stimulation, curiosity, and the desire to transcend oneself. Thus, the infant's mouth projectively identified with mother's breast can create, for instance, a hungry, biting breast, a kissing breast, a scooped-out breast, etc., the latter of which may then be reprojected onto mother as a damaged whole-vagina with teeth, for instance. The infant's hungry eyes can be projectively identified with daddy's penis and then reinternalized as a moralistically voyeuristic superego object. The projective identification of the infant's epistemophilic instinct into the eye of the object (or the reverse, the projective identification of the infant's eyes into mother's mind—then combined with the projective identification of the infant's destructive feelings) can finally cause the internalization of that phenomenon known as "the evil eye"—and so on, and so on.

By and large, the L, H, and K functions produce three normal internal objects: a nurturing object, a protective object (a boundary object or sphincter object: a gatekeeper), and a stimulating object. The pathological vicissitudes of these are many and have been listed. Mason (1981) has discussed the suffocating superego, which is a projective identification of the infant's possessiveness into a breast which is then internalized as a claustrophobia-inducing object which suffocates the life out of the patient's ego.

Internal objects formed by splitting and projective identification constitute, as I stated above, a scaffolding for primitive psychic structure. They correspond to self-objects. It could be said that they are like the baby teeth which await the development of permanent teeth, corresponding to object representations which take their place. Object representations are not internal objects, but rather are the imaginative portraitures of external persons who are no longer possessed by omnipotent desire plus the shadow of the former presence of internal objects. They constitute permanent psychic structures.

The dual-track bids that the therapist/parent extend safety and empathy to the infant/patient while at the same time encouraging the patient to extend amnesty toward him-/herself (self as object). Empathy toward the struggling authentic self must be tempered by vigilance, discipline, and rigor in protecting it from the other split-off, malevolent, but hapless subpersonalities within the psyche whose imaginative births owe their origins to unbearable experience once upon a time. The rigor and discipline with which the therapist and patient must detect and confront these splits must be tempered by the amnesty extended toward their rehabilitation back into psychic at-onement. All this is done so that the infant/patient can utilize his/her own dual-track in confronting the Cafeteria of Experience in order to locate and select those qualities from persons in this world of experience that are needed for survival and for the future, and to separate off those persons and experiences which are not relevant and meaningful to his/her scenario.

Splitting and projective identification have an epigenesis and eventually become sublimated functions within the mature psychic structure. Whereas splitting is to become discrimination and normal porous repression, projective identification not only participates in normal porous repression, but also becomes the means of communication between oneself and oneself and between oneself and the other. In the depressive position of separation-individuation with rapprochement, the infant learns projectively to identify in its mother the feeling of subjectivity so that mother now becomes not only an object but also a co-subject. This is the beginning of empathy in the capacity to tolerate another scenario in a cosmos vaster than the infant's own omnipotent cosmos.

Projective identification ultimately is the basis for thinking. We first become aware of thoughts and feelings as they emerge and/or irrupt into our awareness. Bion calls these "thoughts without a thinker." Freud designated them by a more mechanistic terminology as instinctual drives. I prefer the former. The "thoughts without a thinker" emerge into our awareness for our mind to think about. In order for them to emerge, they must experience a projective trajectory onto the surface of object representations which constitute a table for thought, having been honed from experience with a containing mother who can reflect, "catch," and sort out. This is the basis for a "thinking couple." Ultimately, projective identification, in its most basic communicative form, is the cry of agony of the infant who must put its experience into the caretaking object so that that object can know how the infant feels.

Thus, projective identification has a significance beyond simple communication and can be likened to a spiritual experience. Every culture since the beginning of time has practiced one form or another of ritual sacrifice. The circumcision of the Jews and their kosher ceremonies reflect an even more ancient and more deadly origin. The Christian Eucharist is currently the most well-known ceremony commemorating the mystical need for human sacrifice where the one is chosen as a token to reflect and represent the sacrifices of the many. It seems we are still in that stage of evolution where human sacrifice is needed. The infant may need its mother, father, or sibling to be its own token sacrifice where it can project its agony into these objects so that they can "know" its agony and thereby relieve it. By the same token, parents do likewise with each other and with their children. It is as if all human beings, parents and children alike, are really children who wish someone to know their agony so that the tale can be told. The transmission of this message is projective identification. The capacity to "know" that message is the ability to tolerate suffering through this "exchange transfusion" between the sacred and the profane.

Summary

I have examined the phenomenon of splitting from the standpoint of the subject, verb, and object of its experience. The subject refers to the "I" who splits its experience according to a Cartesian artifice. The verb experience of splitting is the phenomenon of cleaving aspects of "I" and the objects of experience into units for understanding, defense, and action. The object of splitting is the self (the mirror of "I") and "I's" objects. The first experience of splitting is the awareness of nonseparation from the Background Object of Primary Identification.

I further hypothesized there to be a general split of two orders: *(a)* the split between the experience of a primary separate "I" and the continuation of primary identification (self-object presentation); and *(b)* the split between "I" and self (dual-track theory).

I hope to have demonstrated that splitting adumbrates functions of discrimination and of repression. Abnormally, it functions as an attack against thought and perceptual linkages and causes abnormal cleavages between objects and their relationships to self.

I have suggested that dissociated aspects of the personality (molar splits as well as molecular splits) are functions of the installation of a defective Background Object of Primary Identification (a defective primary self-object), the forerunner of subsequent internal objects. If defective, the subsequent history of the personality is destined to experience fragmentation or dissociated states without an overall organization or unity. Associated with the defective Background Object of Primary Identification is the phantasy of the unborn twin which also corresponds to derivatives of the ego-ideal on one hand and the imaginary twin of childhood on the other. I believe the unborn twin and its derivatives to be the organized centrum for later dissociated personality experiences.

I have discussed several features of dissociation of the personality and have suggested that the organizing function of the ego, which correlates with the nonanatomical third brain, applies a synthetic binocularization to anatomical and behavioral splits in the personality. It is the absence of this organization, both neurologically and psychologically, which permits the experience of overt dissociation. I further postulate that all personalities exist in splits or dissociations, but the Background Object of Primary Identification and the normal repressive barrier mitigate their appearance. Borderline and psychotic patients may experience definitive, polarizing splits, splintering or fragmentation, or subtle amorphous disconnectedness. Manic-depressive illness tends to sponsor the polarizing ego-dystonic splits, particularly of the borderline states, whereas schizophrenic illness may usually be responsible for ego-dystonic fragmentation and ego-syntonic amorphousness. *The term "splits" denotes separate subpersonality organizations within the psyche which operate overtly, covertly, simultaneously, sequentially, or alternately. Clinically, we are less aware of their independent existence because of the organizing, integrating, and rectifying capacity of the ego. Generally, we observe them compositely as a montage. Otherwise, it would be like double vision.*

Splitting is a fact of human mental life, and it is reinforced by projective identification. The goal of analysis is to gather the splits and allow a coherence of an at-one-ment.

Projective identification, along with splitting, is the fundamental ingredient in all defense mechanisms and also is the principal instrument of perception, cognition, and object relations. It is the Ariadne's thread in the labyrinth of the internal world and is the architect of its structure. It is a prime component of primary process (with splitting) and is also an important ingredient in secondary process as well. All projection is projective identification since projection is unthinkable without *(a)* identity of self being included in the projection, and *(b)* an acknowledgment of identification secondarily with the projection or a disavowal of identification with the projection—the latter of which is a negative identification with the projection nevertheless.

Whereas splitting is a mechanism which corresponds to the principle of distinction, projective identification is a mechanism which corresponds to the principle of generalization insofar as it brings self and object together and object and object together. It corresponds to Freud's conception of condensation.

I have arbitrarily assumed that externalization applies to those aspects of projective identification which are nondefensive, whereas projective identification proper includes all defensive operations. Thus, disavowal of identification with the projection would constitute defensive projective identification, and acceptance of the identification with projection would constitute externalization. Externalization includes foraging, scanning, exploring, generalizing, imagining, translocating, creating "projects," etc. Defensive projective identification includes *(a)* evacuation of accretions of mental stimuli; *(b)* de-differentiating attainment of "at-one-ment" either with the Background Object of Primary Identification or with a secondary interpersonal object (self-object); and *(c)* the entry of the self into an object in order to control it for omnipotently adaptive purposes. In analysis we make use of the externalizing aspects of projective identification in free association, but we also observe projective identification as the instrument for all phantasies. Thus it is responsible for the creation of the objects which comprise the inner world. Imagination is the metaphor for projective identification.

In analysis we also use projective identification, not only in its function as the agent of the principle of generalization, but also in its capacity to be the instrument of our empathic feelings. Along with splitting, as the agent of intuition and imagination it makes use of the primary process modalities of metonymy, synecdoche, and metathesis to give us a mythical or thoughtful "rewrite" of our thoughts and the thoughts of others.

The phenomenon of projective identification is best understood by the application of the dual-track principle involving the symbiotic, "siamese twin" model in which there can be two states of mind simultaneously on different levels: one of separateness and the other of fusion. Thus, the infant can go back and forth between the two states or experience both states simultaneously. At the same time, this model allows for the infant to experience identification with the projection into the object and also to be able to deny it (disidentification). Projective identification is an object relationship and involves an extension of self into the object rather than a hurling of content into space. In psychosis, projective identification *seems* to be extending the self into an object, but it actually is a withdrawal of self away from its ego boundaries (including mind and sense organs) which then fuse with the object(s) interfacing with that boundary.

Existentially, projective identification is that state of mind (or mindlessness) in which we conduct much of our lives—for we are all "sleepwalkers" more than we realize, and, in the act of trying to be our separate individual selves, we forget how much we walk in the shadow or even in the substance of others. Ultimately, it becomes the task of the patient's understanding of his experience of projective identification to resolve his battle with persecutors so that he may truly know his friends and be able to copy his *true* enemies. The confusion between persecutor and enemy may be one of the deepest causes of emotional impotence.

Transference, rather than merely being a distortion of experience, represents the quintessence of projective identification in its capacity to protectively transfer mental pain from the self to the therapist in a special kind of "siamese" bonding which allows for an "exchange transfusion" between the sacred and the profane. The conduit of that bonding is the therapeutic alliance; the thrust of its viability is projective identification.

References

Berg, M. (1977). The externalizing transference. *International Journal of Psycho-Analysis* 58:235-245.

Bergman, P., and Escalona, S. (1949). Unusual sensitivities in very young children. *Psychoanalytic Study of the Child* 3/4: 333-352.

Bick, E. (1968). The experience of the skin in early object relations. *International Journal of Psycho-Analysis* 4a: 484-486.

Bion, W. (1950). The imaginary twin. In W. Bion, *Second Thoughts*, pp. 3-22. New York: Jason Aronson, 1967.

———— (1953). Notes on the theory of schizophrenia. In *Second Thoughts*, pp. 23-35.

———— (1956). Development of schizophrenic thought. In *Second Thoughts*, pp. 36-42.

———— (1957a) Differentiation of the psychotic from the non-psychotic personalities. In *Second Thoughts*, pp. 43-64.

———— (1957b) On arrogance. In *Second Thoughts*, pp. 86-92.

———— (1958). On hallucination. In *Second Thoughts*, pp. 65-85.

———— (1959a). Attacks on linking. In *Second Thoughts*, pp. 93-109.

———— (1959b). *Experience in Groups*. London: Tavistock.

———— (1962a). A theory of thinking. In *Second Thoughts*, pp. 110-119.

———— (1962b). *Learning from Experience*. In *Seven Servants: Four Works by Wilfred R. Bion*. New York: Jason Aronson, 1977.

———— (1963). *Elements of Psycho-Analysis*. In *Seven Servants*.

———— (1965). *Transformations*. In *Seven Servants*.

———— (1967). *Second Thoughts*. New York: Jason Aronson.

———— (1970). *Attention and Interpretation*. In *Seven Servants*.

Bleuler, E. (1911). *Dementia Praecox*. New York: International Universities Press, 1950.

Bowlby, J. (1958). The nature of the child's tie to his mother. *International Journal of Psycho-Analysis* 39:350–373.

Bradlow, P. (1973). Depersonalization, ego splitting, non-human fantasy and shame. *International Journal of Psycho-Analysis* 54:487–492.

Breuer, J., and Freud, S. (1893–1895). Studies in hysteria. *Standard Edition* 2.

Capgras, J., and Reboul-Lachaux, J. (1923). Illusion des sosies dans un delire systematique chronique. *Bulletin de la Societé* Clinique de Medicine Mentale 11:6–16.

Dorpat, T. (1979). Is splitting a defence? *International Review of Psycho-Analysis* 6:105–115.

Epstein, L., and Feiner, A. H. (1979). Countertransference: the therapist's contribution to treatment. *Contemporary Psychoanalysis.* 15:489–513.

Erikson, E. (1959). *Identity and the Life Cycle.* New York: International Universities Press.

Fairbairn, W. (1940). Schizoid factors in the personality. In W. Fairbairn, *Psychoanalytic Studies of the Personality,* pp. 3–27. London: Tavistock, 1952.

—— (1941). A revised psychopathology of the psychoses and psychoneuroses. In *Psychoanalytic Studies of the Personality,* pp. 28–58.

—— (1943). The repression and the return of the bad objects (with special reference to the 'war neuroses.'). In *Psychoanalytic Studies of the Personality,* pp. 59–81.

—— (1944). Endopsychic structure considered in terms of object relationships. In *Psychoanalytic Studies of the Personality,* pp. 82–136.

—— (1946). Object relationships and dynamic structure. In *Psychoanalytic Studies of the Personality,* pp. 137–151

—— (1949). Steps of the development of an object-relations theory of the personality. In *Psychoanalytic Studies of the Personality,* pp. 152–161.

—— (1952). *Psychoanalytic Studies of the Personality.* London: Tavistock.

—— (1954). *An Object Relations Theory of the Personality.* New York: Basic Books.

Federn, P. (1952). *Ego Psychology and the Psychoses.* New York: Basic Books.

Feigenbaum, D. (1936). On projection. *Psychoanalytic Quarterly* 5:303–319.

Ferenczi, S. (1930). Each adaptation is preceded by an inhibited attempt at splitting. In *Problems and Methods of Psychoanalysis,* pp. 220–221. New York: Basic Books.

Freud, A. (1936). *The Ego and the Mechanisms of Defence.* New York: International Universities Press.

Freud, S. (1893). On the psychical mechanism of hysterical phenomena. *Standard Edition* 3:25–42.

———— (1895). Draft H. *Standard Edition* 1:206–212.

———— (1896). Further remarks on the neuro-psychoses of defence. *Standard Edition* 3:157–185.

———— (1908). Family romances. *Standard Edition* 9:235–241.

———— (1909). Five lectures on psycho-analysis. *Standard Edition* 9:235–241.

———— (1911). Psychoanalytic notes on an autobiographical account of a case of paranoia. *Standard Edition* 12:1–82.

———— (1912). Totem and taboo. *Standard Edition* 13:1–163.

———— (1914a). On the history of the psycho-analytic movement. *Standard Edition* 14:1–66.

———— (1914b). On narcissism: an introduction. *Standard Edition* 14:67–102.

———— (1915a). Instincts and their vicissitudes. *Standard Edition* 14:109–140.

———— (1915b). The unconscious. *Standard Edition* 14:159–215.

———— (1917a). A metapsychological supplement to the theory of dreams. *Standard Edition* 14:217–235.

———— (1917b). Mourning and melancholia. *Standard Edition* 14:237–260.

———— (1919). The 'uncanny.' *Standard Edition* 17:217–256.

———— (1920). Beyond the pleasure principle. *Standard Edition* 18:1–64.

———— (1921). Group psychology and the analysis of the ego. *Standard Edition* 18:65–143.

———— (1922). Some neurotic mechanisms in jealousy, paranoia, and homosexuality. *Standard Edition* 18:221–282.

———— (1923). The ego and the id. *Standard Edition* 19:1–66.

———— (1924). Neurosis and psychosis. *Standard Edition* 19:183–190.

—— (1927). Fetishism. *Standard Edition* 21:149–158.

—— (1933). New introductory lectures on psycho-analysis. *Standard Edition* 22:1–182.

—— (1939). Moses and monotheism. *Standard Edition* 23:1–137.

—— (1940a). An outline of psycho-analysis. *Standard Edition* 23:139–207.

—— (1940b). Splitting of the ego in the process of defence. *Standard Edition* 23:275–278.

Gazzaniga, M., and LeDoux, J. (1978). *The Integrated Mind.* New York: Plenum Press.

Gill, M. (1963). *Topography and Systems in Psychoanalytic Theory.* New York: International Universities Press.

Green, A. (1977). The borderline concept. In *Borderline Personality Disorders,* ed. P. Harticollis, pp. 15–44. New York: International Universities Press.

Greenacre, P. (1941). The predisposition to anxiety. In *Trauma, Growth, and Personality,* pp. 27–82. New York: International Universities Press, 1952.

Grinberg, L. (1962). On a specific aspect of counter-transference due to the patient's projective identification. *International Journal of Psycho-Analysis* 43:436–440.

Grotstein, J. (1977a). The psychoanalytic conept of schizophrenia: I. the dilemma. *International Journal of Psycho-Analysis* 58:403–425.

—— (1977b). The psychoanalytic concept of schizophrenia: II. reconciliation. *International Journal of Psycho-Analysis* 58:427–452.

—— (1978). Inner space: its coordinates and its dimensions. *International Journal of Psycho-Analysis* 59:55–61.

—— (1979a). The significance of Kleinian contributions to psychoanalysis. I. Kleinian instinct theory; II. A comparison between Freudian and Kleinian conceptions of the development of early mental life. *International Journal of Psychoanalytic Psychotherapy.* In press.

—— (1979b). Gradients in analyzability. *International Journal of Psychoanalytic Psychotherapy* 7:137–151.

—— (1979c). The infantile psychosis and the dual-track principle. In press.

—— (1979d). Demoniacal possession, splitting, and the torment of hope. *Contemporary Psychoanalysis* 15:407–445.

———— (1979e). The psychoanalytic concept of the borderline organization. In *Advances in Psychotherapy of the Borderline Patient*, ed. J. LeBoit and A. Capponi., pp. 149–183. New York: Jason Aronson.

———— (1979f). The soul in torment: a newer and older view of psychopathology. *The Bulletin for Catholic Psychiatrists*

———— (1979g). Who is the dreamer who dreams the dream and who is the dreamer who understands it? *Contemporary Psychoanalysis* 15:110–169.

———— (1980a). Autoscopic phenomena. In *Extraordinary Symptoms in Psychiatry*, ed. Claude Friedmann and Robert Faguet. New York: Plenum Press. In press.

———— (1980b). Technical considerations in the analysis of a borderline patient. In *Technical Aspects of Treating Disturbed Patients*, ed. L. Bryce Boyer and Peter L. Giovacchini. In press.

———— (1980c). Towards the decipherment of the schizophrenic experience: a commentary on Ping-Nie Pao's *Schizophrenic Disorders*, at the request of the editors of *Psychoanalytic Inquiry*. To be published in Volume 1, Number 1, Fall, 1980.

———— (1980d). A proposed revision of the psychoanalytic concept of primitive mental states: I. Introduction to a newer psychoanalytic metapsychology; II. The borderline syndrome: disorders of autistic (autotaxic) narcissism in which there is a failure in the quest for safety; III. Self (narcissistic) disorders: disorders of symbiotic (paratoxic) narcissism in which there is a failure in the quest for self-affirmation. *Contemporary Psychoanalysis*. In press.

———— (1980e). The infantile neurosis, the infantile psychosis, and the dual-track principle. *Contemporary Psychoanalysis* Manuscript submitted for publication.

Heimann, P. (1952). Certain functions in introjection and projection in early infancy. In *Developments in Psycho-Analysis,* ed. M. Klein, P. Heimann, J. Riviere, pp. 122–168. London: Hogarth Press.

Horowitz, M. (1976). Cognitive and interactive aspects of splitting. *American Journal of Psychiatry* 134:549–623.

Jacques, E. (1970). *Work, Creativity and Social Justice.* New York: International Universities Press.

Jung, C. G. (1939). On the psychogenesis of schizophrenia. In the *Collected Works of C. G. Jung*, vol. 3, pp. 233–249. Princeton, N.J.: Princeton University Press.

Katan, M. (1954). The importance of the non-psychotic part of the personality in schizophrenia. *International Journal of Psycho-Analysis* 35:119–128.

——— (1964). Fetishism, splitting of the ego, and denial. *International Journal of Psycho-Analysis* 45:237–245.

Kernberg, O. (1975). *Borderline Conditions and Pathological Narcissism.* New York: Jason Aronson.

——— (1976). *Object Relations Theory and Clinical Psychoanalysis.* New York: Jason Aronson.

Klein, M. (1921). The development of a child. In *Contributions to Psycho-Analysis, 1921–1945.* London: Hogarth Press, 1948.

——— (1929). Personification in the play of children. In *Contributions to Psycho-Analysis, 1921–1945.*

——— (1932). *The Psycho-Analysis of Children.* New York: Delacorte, 1975.

——— (1935). A contribution to the psychogenesis of manic-depressive states. In *Contributions to Psycho-Analysis, 1921–1945,* pp. 282–310.

——— (1940). Mourning and its relation to manic-depressive states. In *Contributions to Psycho-Analysis, 1921–1945,* pp. 311–338.

——— (1945). The oedipus complex in the light of early anxieties. In *Contributions to Psycho-Analysis, 1921–1945,* pp. 339–390.

——— (1952a). On the theory of anxiety and guilt. In *Developments in Psychoanalysis,* ed. M. Klein, P. Heimann, J. Riviere, pp. 271–291. London: Hogarth Press.

——— (1952b). Some theoretical conclusions regarding the emotional life of the infant. In *Developments in Psycho-Analysis,* pp. 198–236.

——— (1952c). Notes on some schizoid mechanisms. In *Developments in Psycho-Analysis,* pp. 292–320.

——— (1957a). On identification. In *New Directions in Psychoanalysis,* ed. M. Klein, P. Heimann, R. Money-Kryle, pp. 309–345. New York: Basic Books.

——— (1957b). *Envy and Gratitude.* New York: Basic Books.

——— (1960). *Narrative of a Child Analysis.* New York: Delacorte Press, 1975.

Kohut, H. (1971). *The Analysis of the Self.* New York: International Universities Press.

——— (1977). *The Restoration of the Self.* New York: International Universities Press.

Laing, R. D. (1960). *The Divided Self.* London: Tavistock.

Langs, R. (1976). *The Bipersonal Field.* New York: Jason Aronson.
——— (1978). Some communicative properties of the bipersonal field. *International Journal of Psychoanalytic Psychotherapy* 7:89–136.
Lansky, M. (1974). Delusions in a patient with Capgras' syndrome. *Bulletin of the Menninger Clinic* 38:360–364.
Lichtenberg, J., and Slap, J. (1973). Notes on the concept of splitting and the defense mechanism of the splitting of representations. *Journal of the American Psychoanalytic Association* 21:772–787.
McLaughlin, J.T. (1978). Primary and secondary process in the context of cerebral hemispheric specialization. *Psychoanalytic Quarterly* 47:237–266.
Mahler, M. (1968). *On Human Symbiosis and the Vicissitudes of Individuation.* New York: International Universities Press.
——— (1971). A study of the separation-individuation process and its possible application to borderline phenomena in the psychoanalytic situation. *Psychoanalytic Study of the Child* 26:403–424.
Mahler, M., and Gosliner, B. (1955). On symbiotic child psychoses. *Psychoanalytic Study of the Child* 10:195–212.
Mahler, M., Pine, F., and Bergman, A. (1975). *The Psychological Birth of the Human Infant.* New York: Basic Books.
Malin, A., and Grotstein, J. (1966). Projective identification in the therapeutic process. *International Journal of Psycho-Analysis* 47:26–31.
Mason, A. (1981). The suffocating superego. In *Do I Dare Disturb the Universe? A Memorial for Wilfred R. Bion* ed. J.S. Grotstein, Beverly Hills: Caesura Press.
Masterson, J., and Rinsley, D. (1975). The borderline syndrome: the role of the mother in the genesis and psychic structure of the borderline personality. *International Journal of Psycho-Analysis* 56:163–177.
Meissner, W. W. (1980). A note on projective identification. *Journal of the American Psychoanalytic Association* 28:43–68,
Meltzer, D. (1967). *The Psycho-Analytic Process.* London: Heinemann.
——— (1974). Mutism in infantile autism, schizophrenia, and manic-depressive states. *International Journal of Psycho-Analysis* 55:397–404.
——— (1975). Adhesive identification. *Contemporary Psychoanalysis* 11:289–310.

Meltzer, D., Bremner, J., Hoxter, S., Weddell, D., and Wittenberg, I. (1975). *Explorations in Autism*. Perthshire: Clunie Press.

Novick, J., and Kelly, K. (1970). Projection and externalization. *Psychoanalytic Study of the Child* 25:69–98.

Nunberg, H. (1920). On the catatonic attack. In H. Nunberg, *Practice and Theory of Psychoanalysis*, pp. 3–23. New York: Nervous and Mental Disease Monographs, 1948.

——— (1921). The course of the libidinal conflict in a case of schizophrenia. In *Practice and Theory of Psychoanalysis*, pp. 24–59.

Ogden, T. (1978). A developmental view of identifications resulting from maternal impingements. *International Journal of Psychoanalytic Psychotherapy* 7:486–508.

——— (1979). On projective identification. *International Journal of Psycho-Analysis* 60:357–373.

Ornston, D. (1978a). Projective identification and internal impingement. *International Journal of Psychoanalytic Psychotherapy* 7:508–533.

——— (1978b). On projection: a study of Freud's usage. *Psychoanalytic Study of the Child* 33:117–166.

Paul, M., and Carson, I. (1978). A contribution to the study of dimension. *International Journal of Psycho-Analysis* 7:101–112.

Peto, A. (1977). A model of archaic thinking based on two formulations of Freud. *International Journal of Psycho-Analysis* 58:333–344.

Piaget, J. (1952). *The Origins of Intelligence in Children*. New York: International Universities Press.

Pruyser, P. (1975). What splits in 'splitting'? A scrutiny of the concepts of splitting in psychoanalysis and psychiatry. *Bulletin of the Menninger Clinic* 39:1–46.

Racker, H. (1968). *Transference and Counter-Transference*. London: Hogarth Press.

Rank, O. (1914). *The Double*. Chapel Hill, N.C.: University of North Carolina Press, 1976.

Rosenfeld, H. (1949). Remarks on the relation of male homosexuality to paranoia, paranoid anxiety, and narcissism. In H. Rosenfeld, *Psychotic States*, pp. 13–33. New York: International Universities Press.

——— (1950). Notes on the psychoanalysis of the superego conflict in an acute schizophrenic patient. In *Psychotic States*, pp. 63–103.

——— (1952). Transference-phenomena and transference-analysis in acute schizophrenic patients. In *Psychotic States*, pp. 104–116.

————(1964) An investigation into the need of neurotic and psychotic patients to act out during analysis. In *Psychotic States*, pp. 200–216.

————(1965). *Psychotic States*. New York: International Universities Press.

———— (1971). Contribution to the psychopathology of psychotic states. In *Problems of Psychosis*, ed. P. Doucet, and C. Laurin. Amsterdam: Excerpta Medica.

———— (1978). Notes on the psychopathology and psychoanalytic treatment of some borderline patients. *International Journal of Psycho-Analysis* 59:215–223.

Sandler, J. (1960). The background of safety. *International Journal of Psycho-Analysis* 41:352–356.

Sarnoff, C. (1972). The vicissitudes of projection during an analysis encompassing late latency to early adolescence. *International Journal of Psycho-Analysis* 53:515–523.

Schilder, P. (1933). Experiments on imagination, after images, and hallucinations. *American Journal of Psychiatry* 13:597–611.

———— (1935). *The Image and Appearance of the Human Body*. London: Paul, Trench, Trubner.

Schur, M. (1966). *The Id and the Regulatory Principles of Mental Functioning*. New York: International Universities Press.

Searles, H. (1959). Integration and differentiation in schizophrenia: an over-all view. In *Collected Papers on Schizophrenia and Related Subjects*, pp. 317–399. New York: International Universities Press.

Segal, H. (1964). *Introduction to the Work of Melanie Klein*. New York: Basic Books.

Smith, D. (1974). Some functions of projection in the analytic situation. *International Review of Psycho-Analysis* 1:383–389.

Stewart, W. (1970). The split in the ego and the mechanism of disavowal. *Psychoanalytic Quarterly* 30:1–16.

Stierlin, H. (1969). *Conflict and Reconciliation*. New York: Jason Aronson

Tausk, V. (1919). On the origin of the 'influencing machine' in schizophrenia. In *The Psychoanalytic Reader*, ed., R. Fliess. New York: International Universities Press, 1948.

Todd, J., and Dewhurst, K. (1955). The double psychopathology and physiology. *Journal of Nervous and Mental Disease* 122:47.

Wangh, M. (1962). The "evocation of a proxy": a psychological maneuver, its use as a defense, its purpose and genius. *Psychoanalytic Study of the Child* 17:451–469.

Weiss, E. (1947). Projection, extrajection and objectivation. *Psychoanalytic Quarterly* 16:357–377.

Winnicott, D. (1948). Paediatrics and psychiatry. In *Collected Papers,* pp. 157–173. New York: Basic Books, 1958.

————— (1950). Aggression in relation to emotional development. In *Collected Papers,* pp. 204–218.

————— (1952). Psychoses and child care. In *Collected Papers,* pp. 219–228.

————— (1960). The theory of the parent-infant relationship. In *The Maturational Processes and the Facilitating Environment,* pp. 37–55. New York: International Universities Press, 1965.

————— (1963). Communicating and not communicating leading to a study of certain opposites. In *The Maturational Processes and the Facilitating Environment,* pp. 179–192.

————— (1965). *The Maturational Processes and the Facilitating Environment.* New York: International Universities Press.

Wolheim, R. (1969). The mind and the mind's image of itself. *International Journal of Psycho-Analysis* 50:209–220.

Wynne, L., and Singer, M. (1963a). Thought disorders and family relations of schizophrenics. I. a research strategy. *Archives of General Psychiatry* 9:191–198.

————— (1963b). Thought disorders and family relations of schizophrenics. II. a classification of forms of thinking. *Archives of General Psychiatry* 9:199–206.

Index